International Praise for
How to Be a Dictator

"An extraordinarily funny study of political thinking, serious beneath the surface, filled with dark humor and remarkable facts."

—*Dagbladet* (Norway)

"A serious subject handled in a most humorous way . . . The details about the reign of small and large lunatics in a number of countries form the substance, but with his special take on the subject and his relaxed, dry humor, the book is very readable. It could just as well be read as a lesson in fun facts before quiz night as it can be a reminder of corruption, murder, and mis-government."

—*Faedrelandsvennen* (Norway)

"Light and entertaining. Lots of facts. You'll want to know more about the dictatorships after reading the book."

—*Finansavisen* (Norway)

"Maybe *How to Be a Dictator* is for more than just laughs. The book is a funny reminder of how depressingly rich our flora of tyrants really is."

—*Klassekampen* (Norway)

"This book lets you know what to do to climb to the top—and stay there. Useful advice and guidelines to avoid trouble are also included. Humorous!"

—*Tønsberg Blad* (Norway)

HOW TO BE A
DICTATOR

HOW TO BE A
DICTATOR

AN IRREVERENT GUIDE

MIKAL HEM

TRANSLATED FROM THE NORWEGIAN
BY KERRI PIERCE

Arcade Publishing • New York

First English-language Edition

This edition is published by agreement with Kontext Agency.
Originally published in Norway in 2012 by Pax Forlag under the title *Kanskje jeg kan bli diktator*.

Arcade Publishing books may be purchased in bulk at special discounts for sales promotion, corporate gifts, fund-raising, or educational purposes. Special editions can also be created to specifications. For details, contact the Special Sales Department, Arcade Publishing, 307 West 36th Street, 11th Floor, New York, NY 10018 or arcade@skyhorsepublishing.com.

Arcade Publishing® is a registered trademark of Skyhorse Publishing, Inc.®, a Delaware corporation.

Visit our website at www.arcadepub.com.

10 9 8 7 6 5 4 3 2 1

Names: Hem, Mikal, 1973- author. | Pierce, Kerri A., translator.
Title: How to be a dictator : an irreverent guide / Mikal Hem ; translated from the Norwegian by Kerri Pierce.
Other titles: Kanskje jeg kan bli diktator. English
Description: New York : Skyhorse Publishing, Inc., [2017] | Includes bibliographical references.
Identifiers: LCCN 2017002215 (print) | LCCN 2017013312 (ebook) | ISBN 9781628726619 (ebook) | ISBN 9781628726602 (hardcover : alk. paper)
Subjects: LCSH: Dictatorship. | Dictators.
Classification: LCC JC495 (ebook) | LCC JC495 .H45 2017 (print) | DDC 321.9—dc23
LC record available at https://lccn.loc.gov/2017002215

Cover design by Erin Seaward-Hiatt
Cover illustration by Andrew Howe/iStockphoto

Printed in the United States of America

CONTENTS

Introduction

THE APPEAL OF DICTATORSHIP

THERE ARE MANY REASONS TO seek power. With power comes influence, control, admiration, and often wealth. Unfortunately, Western democracies place limits on just how much political power you can obtain. Consider the attention democratically elected leaders must pay to their political opposition, not to mention the waffling of voters between candidates. When voters tire of one political leader, they simply elect a new one into office.

Dictators, on the other hand, operate within an entirely different realm. Unburdened by opposing politicians or inquisitive media, dictators are in a much better position to realize their political and personal agenda. You can, for example, amass an enormous fortune, as most dictators do, without the people, the press, or any government agencies being the wiser. And should someone impudently try to shed light on your private affairs, why, you can simply change the law to ensure that such subversive behavior is a punishable offense. That is exactly what Azerbaijan's president, Ilham Aliyev, did in June 2012. Following multiple revelations that the dictator and his family happened to control substantial portions of the country's mining operations, telephone companies, and construction ventures, its parliament adopted laws granting the president and his wife immunity against prosecution for all crimes committed during his tenure. They also adopted a law banning the media from publishing information about the president's business undertakings without explicit consent from those concerned.

And consider this: most people who claim to be God are whisked away for psychiatric treatment. Among dictators, however, it is entirely acceptable to elevate yourself to or juxtapose yourself with the Divine. Rafael Trujillo, former dictator of the Dominican Republic, once erected a large neon sign in Ciudad Trujillo, the capital, that read DIOS Y TRUJILLO, meaning "God and Trujillo." The country's churches were forced to display the slogan DIOS EN CIELO, TRUJILLO EN TIERRA, meaning "God in Heaven, Trujillo on Earth." In neighboring Haiti, François "Papa Doc" Duvalier went a step further and appointed himself the highest deity in that country's Voodoo religion. Ali Soilih, who governed the Comoro Islands for a few years during the 1970s, said: "I am your God and teacher. I am the divine way, the torch that lights the dark. There is no God but Ali Soilih."

While other state heads must consider citizens' wishes before erecting buildings and infrastructure, dictators are not limited by such petty considerations. They can erect enormous towers, monuments, or other vanity structures without worrying about open bidding and voter opinion. Take the Ivory Coast's Félix Houphouët-Boigny, who built the world's largest church in Yamoussoukro. The church has seven thousand seats equipped with embedded air ducts to cool the faithful, though it still remains mostly empty. Saparmurat Niyazov used billions of Turkmenistan's petrodollars to transform the capital into a gleaming city of white marble. Other dictators have gone even further. Than Shwe of Burma and Nursultan Nazarbayev of Kazakhstan each built new capitals from the ground up.

Furthermore, dictators usually occupy power longer than their democratically elected colleagues. The list of heads of state who have been in power the longest is topped by despots. It must be acknowledged, of course, that democrats are more secure at the beginning of their term in office. For the first six months, they have only a 30 percent chance of being replaced—compared to authoritarians, who have almost a 50 percent chance. After this point, however, dictators hold the clear advantage. A democratically elected leader who has lasted the first six months in office has a 43 percent chance of losing his or her job within the next two years, while that chance stands at just 29 percent for authoritarians. Indeed, a measly 4 percent of all democrats manage to stay in power for ten years or more. The odds for dictators are nearly three times as high: 11 percent manage to hold office for a decade or longer.

One of the most amusing things you can do as a dictator is to introduce quirky laws that your subjects must follow. For example, Romania's communist leader, Nicolae Ceaușescu, outlawed typewriting without governmental consent. But some of his most bizarre laws were aimed at increasing Romania's population. Birth control methods were outlawed, and childless women were forced to pay a celibacy tax, even when they weren't to blame for their state. Books on human reproduction and sexuality were considered state secrets and were permissible only as medical textbooks. As the Romanian dictator apparently put it, "The fetus is the property of the entire society. Anyone who avoids having children is a deserter who abandons the laws of national continuity." Ceaușescu also prohibited female news anchors from using makeup on television. Turkmenistan's deceased president, Saparmurat "Turmenbashi" Niyazov, similarly introduced a makeup ban for all female news anchors. The dictator also prohibited lip-synching at all public concerts.

Ayatollah Ruhollah Khomeini took this idea even further. In 1979, following the Iranian Revolution that brought him to power, he outlawed music. As he remarked right after the revolution, "Music stupefies people listening to it and makes their brain inactive and frivolous. . . . If you want independence for your country, you must suppress music and not fear being called old-fashioned." Accordingly, revolutionary guards crawled through people's homes in search of instruments, records, and videotapes.

Yet another advantage of dictatorship is that dictators tend to exhibit exceptional abilities above and beyond governance. Dictators are academic geniuses, brilliant authors, and keen businessmen. They are also particularly talented athletes. For example, in 1994, the North Korean media reported that their Dear Leader, Kim Jong Il, had achieved five holes-in-one in a single round of golf—and that was very the first time he'd played! The dictator finished the eighteen-hole course with a thirty-eight under par.

Not surprisingly, Kim Jong Il was an inspiration to other North Korean athletes. Such was the case for Jong Song-ok, who won the women's marathon in the 1999 World Championships in Athletics in Seville. As she told journalists: "I imagined in my mind the image of our Korean leader, Kim Jong Il, and this inspired me."

Uganda's dictator, Idi Amin, opened the African Amateur Boxing Championships with a fight between himself and

Peter Seruwagi, the trainer for Uganda's national team. Amin achieved an easy victory. In a newspaper the following day, beneath the modest headline "Boxer of the Year," Ugandans could read that "the referee had to stop the fight in the second round to save Seruwagi from further punishment."

Another athletic dictator is Turkmenistan's president, Gurbanguly Berdymukhamedov, who holds, among other things, black belts in taekwondo and karate. When Turkmenistan held its first car race in April 2012, the president decided to drop by. He arrived in a stylish Bugatti Veyron, one of the world's fastest and most expensive cars, and a favorite among the dictator set. After being introduced by the master of ceremonies, Berdymukhamedov asked to participate, and the organizer consented, despite the president's late entry. By chance, the necessary racing gear was available in the president's size, and Berdymukhamedov took his seat in a Turkish Volkicar. The dictator really went for it and achieved the best result in the time-trial challenge. Naturally, the car was donated to the national sports museum after the race.

However, dictatorship isn't all fun and sports for dictators alone; their subjects join in too. In Haiti during the 1960s, under the rule of François "Papa Doc" Duvalier, Haitian roulette was born. The presidential palace in the capital, Port-au-Prince, was surrounded by the president's nervous and trigger-happy guards, who tended to pepper away at anything they considered remotely threatening. Haitian roulette involved driving a car with bad tires at full speed past the presidential palace. A blowout meant you lost.

When it comes to imposing your will, dictators obviously have much greater freedom than their democratic counterparts. Your imagination is the limit. You can, for example, turn personally significant days into national holidays. Iraq's Saddam Hussein was only one of many dictators who turned their birthday into a national holiday. Turkmenistan's Saparmurat Niyazov declared his mother's birthday a national holiday. Valentine Strasser, who was president of Sierra Leone from 1992 to 1996, was more imaginative: he proclaimed Saint Valentine's Day and Bob Marley's birthday to be national holidays. Togo's deceased president, Gnassingbé Eyadéma, miraculously survived a plane crash on January 24, 1974, that killed everyone else on board. Eyadéma had recently argued with a French firm over the rights to a phosphate mine. He claimed, with obvious logic, that the French were behind the tragedy. Luckily, his "magical abilities" saved him, and he transformed January 24 into "The Feast of Victory over Forces of Evil." He also commissioned a comic book that, in addition to recounting the story, featured himself as a superhero.

Eyadéma exhibited another trait common to modern dictators: the perpetual need to be surrounded by women (in recent times, all dictators have been men). As a result, he was never without the group of one thousand women who sang and danced in his honor. Likewise, Libya's Muammar Gadhafi had an all-female bodyguard unit, while Thomas Sankara, the deceased dictator of Burkina Faso, had an all-female security detail whom he outfitted with motorcycles, as he himself was a motorcycle enthusiast.

Dictators are clever when it comes to giving themselves titles. Idi Amin called himself, among other things, "Lord of All the Beasts of the Earth and Fishes of the Seas," "The Last King of Scotland," and "Conqueror of the British Empire in Africa in General and Uganda in Particular." Romania's Ceaușescu titled himself "The Genius of the Carpathians." Muammar

Gadhafi's official title was "Guide of the First of September Great Revolution of the Socialist People's Libyan Arab Jamahiriya," but he was also referred to simply as "Brother, Leader, and Revolution's Guide."

As a dictator, you have the opportunity to accumulate enormous wealth, write bestselling novels, build monuments, palaces, and cities in your honor, enjoy unlimited access to attractive sexual partners, and wallow in luxury. Yet how best to exploit these possibilities? The following chapters offer a guide on how to become and act like a dictator, based on examples taken from some of the best in the business. If you follow the advice contained in this book, you will be well on the road to becoming a notable authoritarian.

HOW TO BE A
DICTATOR

1

HOW TO BECOME A DICTATOR

ON THE NIGHT OF APRIL 12, 1980, Richard William Tolbert, Jr. was fast asleep in his home in Liberia's capital, Monrovia. At that time, Liberia was considered a stable corner of a continent fraught with unrest, civil war, and coups. Tolbert had served as Liberia's president since 1971, when he took over from his predecessor, William Tubman. Tubman had governed the West African country for twenty-seven years before that. Tolbert had no reason to believe that his presidential term would end any time soon.

Liberia was a one-party state, and had been since the country's founding by freed American slaves, the first of whom arrived in 1820. In 1847, the African American settlers declared Liberia an independent country. Since then, an elite group consisting of the freed slaves' descendants had governed Liberia, while the country's native inhabitants had been marginalized. Together with Ethiopia, Liberia is the only African country that has never been a colony.

Early that April morning, Sergeant Samuel Kanyon Doe snuck into Tolbert's house with a handful of officers and soldiers, all members of Liberia's native population. Witnesses have testified that Doe cut out Tolbert's entrails while he slept, and twenty-six of Tolbert's supporters were killed in battle. The erstwhile president's corpse was thrown into a mass grave along with other victims of the coup. On April 22, following brief trials, thirteen ministers were publicly executed. A number of the previous regime's supporters were also arrested.

The coup set in motion a series of events that cast Liberia into twenty-five years of chaos, leading to two civil wars and numerous colorful heads of state.

In order to become a dictator, you obviously must achieve one thing: power. Easier said than done. There are a limited number of countries on Earth and an abundance of people who crave power and political influence. When you consider the way power has changed hands throughout history, the road to the top can be surprisingly simple. An aspiring dictator has several possibilities. Some receive help from foreign actors, while others are democratically elected. Still others achieve power by chance—by having the right parents or simply being in the right place at the right time—while some are pawns in a game without realizing it.

For most dictator hopefuls, seizing control of a country requires hard work and careful planning. Luckily, there are various paths to dictatorship that fit different countries and situations. If you harbor an inner dictator, you should give diligent thought to how you will achieve your dream. History is full of botched attempts, and a botched attempt can quickly send you into exile or, if you're less fortunate, into the grave. Luckily, a number of methods have been tried and tested with time, and a handful have a relatively good success rate.

Once you've set your sights on dictatorship, it becomes a question of where you should proceed. The most natural choice may be your homeland, but the conditions there might not always be favorable. It is significantly more difficult to become dictator of a country deeply rooted in democracy than of those that already host authoritarian regimes. Dictators generally take over from previous dictators, and one despot typically gives way to a new one. Of course, that rule isn't set in stone. Take Latin America, where a number of former dictatorships, such as Argentina and Chile, are now well-established democracies. When it comes to Western Europe, Portugal and Spain were dictatorships not too long ago. The Eastern European dictatorships fell even more recently.

Yet, democracy doesn't always last forever. Vladimir Putin has pulled Russia further away from a well-functioning democracy than it was prior to his tenure. If he doesn't yet warrant the title of absolute dictator, there is much to suggest that such a status is exactly what he has in mind. In recent years, democratically elected leaders in many Latin American countries have granted themselves broader powers and limited the freedom of the press. That doesn't necessarily mean these leaders will become dictators—Latin America, after all, has a tradition of wavering between dictatorship and democracy—but they are certainly moving in the same direction taken by previous despots on a quest for absolute power.

Even in Western Europe, democracy cannot be considered secure and everlasting. Modern representative democracy is a relatively new invention, and it is difficult to know how robust it will prove over long periods. There are also instances where people actually surrender power through the democratic process.

In 2003, an overwhelming majority of Lichtenstein's population voted for a constitution giving the Sovereign Prince power to overrule democratic institutions. The Sovereign Prince can veto any law parliament suggests, and he can dissolve the government or boot the ministers. Although Belarus's president, Aleksandr Lukasjenko, has been called Europe's last dictator, Prince Hans-Adam II of Lichtenstein might not have far to go to double that number.

In sum, there is no reason to abandon your inner dictator. As we shall see, if your goal is to seize control of a country, there are a number of tried-and-true methods out there.

STAGE A COUP

Samuel Doe's power grab in Liberia is a classic coup d'état, or simply coup. A coup implies a rapid seizure of power and is usually carried out by a small group within the existing power structure. Typically speaking, coup makers come from the military.

For the last century, coups have been the most common type of power grab. Many people associate the entire Latin American continent with frequent coups, not without reason. In the last one hundred years, there have been forty-five coups and attempted coups in Paraguay alone. Nonetheless, Paraguay appears the image of stability when compared to Bolivia, which has witnessed around two hundred coups since declaring independence in 1825. That is more than one coup per year! Africa has also been particularly susceptible to coups in the last fifty years. Between 1952 and 2000, eighty-five coups were carried out in thirty-three African countries. Forty-two of these coups occurred in West Africa, where Liberia is situated.

Coups are a popular form of power grab, but this method cannot be employed everywhere. Military historian Edward Luttwork observes that the following three factors must be in place to make a coup possible:

Economic Underdevelopment

Impoverished countries are significantly more coup-friendly than rich countries. Poverty is often associated with low public participation in governmental politics. The population is poorly educated, has a high level of illiteracy, and tends to live outside the cities. Power remains in the hands of a small, educated, and affluent elite. A coup in a country where power changes hands among members of the elite, therefore, will have little significance for the average farmer or industry worker. Having lacked all political influence under the previous government, these people will have little reason to oppose a regime change. In contrast, within countries where political influence is spread among a variety of people and institutions, and where more people have something to protect, coups are more difficult to carry out.

Political Independence

In order for a coup to be successful, your target country must be politically independent. After all, it is impossible to seize power if that power is located elsewhere. During the 1956 Hungarian Revolution, for example, demonstrators seized control of all Hungarian power centers, including the army, the police, and the public broadcasting units. Unfortunately, the real power was not located in Hungry but rather in Moscow, 160 miles away. The Soviet Union had troops stationed in and around Hungary, beyond the control of the new Hungarian power players.

In order for the Hungarian Revolution to have been successful, it needed to have been carried out in Moscow.

Unified Power

To enable a direct seizure of power, power itself must be collected into institutions capable of being centrally coordinated and controlled. If, on the other hand, power is divided among elements that only use the regime as a front, or if it is divided into regional entities that exist independent of some central authority, a coup will be made much more difficult. Early in United States history, when individual states had a significant amount of autonomy, it is questionable whether a coup staged in Washington, DC, would have been successful. In today's Democratic Republic of Congo, the central authority is so weak that a coup staged in the capital, Kinshasa, would not necessarily give you control over other parts of the country. Somalia, for its part, lacks all central authority and is not, therefore, a regime that could fall victim to a coup attempt.

It follows that the perfect candidate for a coup is an impoverished country where power is located in the hands of a small elite that is largely independent of outside influence. When you have found yourself the perfect country, it is high time to begin planning the event itself. You must be clear on who is loyal enough to be involved, who in the existing power structure will support you, and who is not likely to abandon the existing leader. You also have to plan how you'll handle any resistance and how to break the news to the populace. In addition, you must be prepared for other countries' reactions.

Nonetheless, the most important rule of thumb is to have the military on your side. Without military support, a coup is practically impossible.

MUSTER FOREIGN SUPPORT

Mustering foreign support used to be simple. Once upon a time, if you wanted the help of the United States, all you had to do was claim you were trying to prevent the communists from coming to power. Similarly, if you wanted to secure Soviet Union support, you could claim you were fighting the good fight against capitalism. Of course, foreign support can always backfire. When Patrice Lumumba, the first elected prime minster of the newly independent country of Congo, found himself on good footing with the Russians, the Americans became concerned. Larry Devlin, the CIA station chief in the Congo, has described how the CIA attempted to assassinate Lumumba via a poisoned tube of smuggled toothpaste, after which they would have installed their own preferred candidate, Mobutu Sese Seko. Luckily for the Americans, Belgian agents and Congolese dissidents beat them to it. On January 17, 1961, Lumumba was assassinated and dumped in an unmarked grave, allowing Mobutu to come to power after all.

Unfortunately, finding support for your coup is no longer as easy as it was during the Cold War. These days, if you want American help, you need to concoct a story about the targeted regime supporting terrorists. On the other hand, if foreign countries cannot help you, there are always mercenaries.

One of the most active mercenaries after World War II was Frenchman Bob Denard. In the course of his career, Denard fought in Congo, Angola, Yemen, Nigeria, and Iran, among other places, often on behalf of France. One of his favorite locations was the island country of Comoros, just off Africa's east coast, where he participated in four coups. The Comoros is in general a coup-friendly place. Since the country's independence in 1975, there have been more than twenty coups and coup attempts. Right after Comoros declared itself independent, Denard removed President Ahmed Abdallah and replaced him with France's chosen man, Ali Soilih. In 1978, Denard was back in the country, this time with support from Rhodesia and South Africa, neither of whom appreciated the leftist direction Soilih's politics had taken. Along with forty-three soldiers, Denard removed the president and reinstated Abdallah. Soilih was murdered a short time later, presumably by Abdallah's supporters.

Denard then settled in the Comoros and used the country as a base for military operations on the African mainland. For the next decade, he served as chief of the president's bodyguard and as Comoros's de facto leader. However, by 1989, South Africa and France were no longer interested in supporting a mercenary regime. Abdallah was murdered and Denard, who was undoubtedly involved in the assassination, was forced to flee.

In 1995, he was back again. Together with thirty men using inflatable Zodiac boats, Denard entered the country on September 27 and removed President Said Mohamed Djohar. This time, though, France had no intention of letting him escape. On October 3, 1995, French soldiers deployed to the Comoros and arrested Denard. Although he was sentenced to five years in prison for "belonging to a gang who conspired to commit a crime," he died in 2007 before he could atone.

KEY POWER PLAYERS: PATRIOTIC, DEMOCRATIC, AND HETEROSEXUAL

Now that you've secured military and perhaps foreign support, it is time to identify the key power players. Where is the real power located? Who should be arrested? Which components of the police and security forces ought to be neutralized first? It is imperative to achieve control as quickly as possible. The planning must also involve as few people as possible and remain as quiet as possible. If your target's intelligence gets wind of your plans, it is a simple matter to neutralize your coup before it begins.

During the coup itself, you must quickly seize control of radio and television. Once you've come to power, it's customary to give a speech broadcast on radio and television informing the populace of the power shift. One important note: never use the word "coup." Instead, describe your power grab as a "revolution," a fight for human rights, or the resolution of a constitutional crisis. You should also justify your seizure of power with one or more of the following reasons:

We were forced to do it in order to
1. Rid ourselves of corruption and nepotism
2. Protect the constitution
3. Remove a tyrant
4. Introduce democracy

On the morning of April 22, 1990, listeners of the Federal Radio Corporation of Nigeria heard the following official announcement:

> On behalf of the patriotic and well-meaning peoples of the Middle Belt and the southern parts of the country, I, Major Gideon Orkar, wish to happily inform you of the successful ousting of the dictatorial, corrupt, drug-baronish, evil man, deceitful, homosexually-centered, prodigalistic, unpatriotic administration of General Ibrahim Badamosi Babangida.

What a shining summary! In this one paragraph, coup-maker Gideon Orkar succeeds in weaving together the charges of dictatorship, corruption, and drug-dealing (expressed through a fine neologism: "drug-baronish"), not to mention general evil. Even sexual orientation is covered. Unfortunately for Orkar, Igrahin Babangida's regime struck back and crushed the coup. Orkar was duly executed.

Coups, as we see, have long-standing historical traditions. Done right, a coup is a quick and effective means to power. The downside is the price for failure—if your coup fails, most likely your fate will be a dark cell, a long sojourn in another country, or a prompt execution. A coup does not work under all circumstances. Fortunately, there are other ways to the top.

BEER AND SEVERED EARS

The life of the Liberian warlord Charles Taylor resembles a Hollywood action movie. Taylor was born on January 28, 1948, in Arthington, not far from Liberia's capital, Monrovia. In 1972, he left for the United States to study economics. Once there, he became politically engaged, and during a 1979 state visit by then Liberian president William Tolbert, Taylor led a demonstration against Liberia's United Nations delegation in New York. He was later arrested for threatening to take over the UN delegation by force. After that, Taylor traveled back to Liberia, where he supported Samuel Doe's coup against President Tolbert in 1980. As a reward, Taylor was given an important position in Doe's new regime. Taylor squeezed as much money as he could from the position and was fired in 1983 for embezzling almost a million dollars.

Taylor fled back to the United States but was arrested in Massachusetts on May 24, 1984, and sent to prison to await Liberian extradition. In spectacular Beagle Boys style, he and four other inmates succeeded in escaping from their high-security lockup. They sawed through an iron window bar in an unused laundry room, shimmied down a knotted sheet rope, and climbed a fence to freedom.

Although his four fellow prison breakers were subsequently captured, Taylor succeeded in flying the coop. He traveled to Libya, where he received military training from Muammar Gadhafi. After that, he headed to Liberia's neighbor, the Ivory Coast, where he founded the National Patriotic Front of Liberia (NPFL), a guerrilla army. In December 1989, he returned to Liberia to remove Doe from office.

Unfortunately for Taylor, a defector from his own guerrilla army beat him to the punch. In September 1990, his former ally Prince Johnson captured the capital of Monrovia and jailed Doe, who, it turns out, was quite superstitious. Johnson's soldiers removed a number of amulets from Doe, including one sequestered in his anus. A Palestinian journalist was allowed to be present in Johnson's headquarters to film Doe's interrogation. In the video, Doe can be seen sitting in his underwear surrounded by soldiers. Across from him sits an obviously drunk Johnson, sipping from a bottle of Budweiser, with a chain of hand grenades around his neck, while a woman fans him with a hand towel. At one point, Johnson strikes the table with his fist and orders a person to cut off Doe's ear. Several soldiers hold the ex-president down while his ear is removed. In one version of the video, Johnson appears to eat parts of the severed ear. Doe was hauled away and killed, and Johnson declared himself President of Liberia. Afterward, Johnson proudly showed this brutal video to foreign journalists visiting his headquarters, and it was broadcast on television the world over.

Of course, Johnson's presidential term did not last many days, and the Liberian civil war resumed. Even though Johnson himself was unsuccessful, his road to power was a time-honored path. Many of today's sitting dictators started their careers with the weaponized opposition to a ruling regime, an occupying power, or a colonial state.

THE MAO METHOD

Coming to power via guerrilla warfare has its pros and cons. It requires patience—a liberation war, after all, can last decades. It is usually a violent method, with significant numbers of killed and wounded soldiers on both sides, not to mention civilian casualties. There is also a real danger that you will get yourself killed or imprisoned.

On the other hand, guerrilla warfare has a number of advantages. If you lead a guerrilla army to victory, you are all but guaranteed the position of state leader, should you want it. Your own people will hail you as a hero. And if you happen to come from an ethnic majority, your legitimacy as leader will be secured for a long time to come. Furthermore, if the opposing regime is a colonial power, a large empire, or is morally reprehensible, you can secure international hero status. This can provide your campaign with key material and moral support. In addition, it affords you a grace period of "moral superiority," during which it is not considered acceptable to criticize you.

Paul Kagame seized control of Rwanda in 1994 shortly after the previous regime, led by Juvénal Hayarimana, had murdered somewhere between half a million to one million people in the most effective genocide the world had ever seen. Kagame and his guerrilla army, therefore, could reap the honor of having stopped the murders while the international community stood helplessly by. Sure enough, this fact has granted Kagame "moral immunity" that makes it impossible for other countries to criticize him for human rights violations. After all, he can always ask: "Where were you when the worst crimes in Rwanda happened?"—something he regularly does when condemned for his authoritarian leadership.

A guerrilla army also has the advantage of being difficult to suppress, even by a massively superior force. That being said, it is far from certain a guerrilla army will triumph. Before you embark on guerrilla warfare, you must determine if conditions are right for victory and which approach is the most useful. Many things must be in place before you can carry out a successful coup:

A Clear Goal

You must have a clear goal for your action. That goal can be leading the fight against an oppressive regime, against an occupying power, or in the name of a political ideology. Clear goals muster your allies, make it easier for you to achieve popular support, and inspire your soldiers for the long struggle ahead.

Broad Support

You want to have support from broad sections of the populace. Therefore, the opposing regime should be unpopular. That regime can be an occupying foreign power, a tyrannical leader, or an ethnic minority.

International Supporters

Having international sympathy for your cause also helps. This sympathy can be attained through good marketing techniques and a strong lobbying network. Foreign supporters can collect money, help secure weapons, and apply pressure to the existing regime. Having a friendly government in a neighboring country is also an advantage. This provides you a place of retreat and a route to transport of weapons and supplies.

Military Advantage

At first glance, a guerrilla army is seemingly no match for a larger and better-equipped national army. Nonetheless, a guerrilla army can have the military advantage for many reasons. If the current regime is unpopular, government soldiers will hardly be motivated to do a good job. If the war drags on, they can become fatigued. A guerrilla army, on the other hand, is typically far more robust than most military troops.

Not all these contingencies have to be in place in order to achieve victory in a guerrilla war. Kagame, for example, did not enjoy broad support among the Rwandese populace when he came to power in 1994. He was, after all, a member of an ethnic minority that comprised only about 15 percent of the country's population. However, he had the clear goal of stopping the oppression (and eventually the genocide) of thousands, he fought against a murderous and despotic regime, he had support from neighboring Uganda, and his army was extremely disciplined and capable. Isaias Afwerki, for his part, fought a heroic liberation war against Ethiopia with almost no international support, not to mention a substantial military disadvantage. Nonetheless, the desire for independence was so strong among both the populace and the guerrilla soldiers that they endured thirty years of liberation warfare before Eritrea became an independent dictatorship in 1993.

Mao Zedong's approach is also worth noting. He led a successful guerrilla war and ended up as China's dictator. In his book *On Guerrilla Warfare*, Mao describes the three stages of a successful guerrilla war. The first stage is a propaganda campaign directed at the populace in order to muster support for your cause. The second stage is a targeted campaign against military installations, strategically important infrastructure, and political objectives. This stage is designed to weaken and demotivate the enemy, while garnering support through a show of strength. The third stage employs conventional warfare techniques for capturing cities, toppling the regime, and taking control of the country. This chronology, of course, is not set in stone. A person can hop back and forth among phases as needed, and they don't need to maintain the same tempo in all parts of the country at once. Not surprisingly, Mao's theories of guerrilla warfare have been read by guerrilla leaders the world over. They were successfully employed by the Vietcong against American troops during the Vietnam War and by Robert Mugabe in Rhodesia, among others.

Achieving power after a liberation war gives you an obvious advantage. You are almost guaranteed to win the first post-victory election. This fact, combined with your aforementioned moral superiority, gives you a very promising start on your way to dictatorship.

Take Robert Mugabe. Like many other post–World War II African intellectuals, Mugabe engaged in anticolonial activity. He was arrested by Rhodesian authorities and imprisoned for a decade. In 1965, Rhodesia declared its independence. The country was an international pariah, an apartheid nation, where blacks did not have the same rights as whites. As such, no country would recognize Rhodesia's independence. Inspired by Mao, both politically and militarily, Mugabe continued the war, and in 1979, the white minority government surrendered. The year 1980 saw the first free election in what is now Zimbabwe. Mugabe's party, ZANU, won with 63 percent of the vote, and Mugabe became the prime minister while the whole world stood at his back.

Mugabe immediately began disposing of his rivals. After dissent from the inhabitants of Matabeleland—which belonged to the Ndebele tribe, in contrast to Mugabe's Shona tribe—the new prime minster dispatched his famous Fifth Brigade. These were elite soldiers trained in North Korea. The result: more than twenty thousand people killed and thousands more sent to concentration camps and tortured. The operation was given the poetic name Gukurahundi, which in Shona loosely means "the early rain which washes away the chaff before the spring rains."

The Zimbabwe authorities attempted to keep Operation Gukurahundi secret from the general populace and foreigners. Even though isolated diplomats and journalists knew what had occurred, relatively little was made public. Mugabe's initiative during the liberation war ensured he retained hero status both at home and abroad until well into the 1990s. At that point, Mugabe was already a firmly entrenched dictator.

A SPLENDID CAMPAIGN

After Prince Johnson killed Doe, Liberia's civil war became an increasingly chaotic fight between various guerrilla forces. Officially, the civil war ended in 1995, after lengthy negotiations. In 1997, the first election was held, and Charles Taylor lost no time in declaring himself a presidential candidate.

No one can accuse Taylor of campaigning dishonestly. He ran for election under a fitting slogan—"He killed my ma, he killed my pa, but I will vote for him"—and secured an overwhelming 75 percent of the vote. What especially prompted the landslide was the fear that Taylor would start another civil war if he lost. Ellen Johnson Sirleaf, who would later be elected president and awarded the Nobel Peace Prize, received only 10 percent of the vote.

As Taylor's victory demonstrates, the path to dictatorship is not necessarily a violent one. It is entirely possible to be democratically elected, only to become a dictator later. For liberation heroes, it is no great leap from military victory to election victory. You can also win that first election by ordinary means, without a guerrilla war. Of course, before you actually sit in power, your ability to tamper with election results is limited. That possibility becomes yours only when you're the one organizing the election, which we will return to in the next chapter.

DREAMS OF DISNEYLAND

Many of today's dictators became heads of state with little to no effort—they simply inherited the position. Indeed, one of the surest paths to dictatorship is to have a dictator dad, and inheriting power is an old and respected tradition. In countries like Norway, the tradition is observed only symbolically and the royal family has no true power, but there are a number of absolute monarchies on Earth.

Azerbaijan's current president, Ilham Alijev, took over from his father, Heydar Alijev, in 2003. Bashar Assad became president of Syria when his father, Hafez Assad, died in 2000 after governing the country for twenty-nine years. In Gabon, Ali Bongo Ondimba became president when his father, Omar Bongo, died in 2009. When Toto's president Gnassingbé Eyadéma died in 2005, his son, Faure Gnassingbé, was named his successor. Following pressure from neighboring countries, Gnassingbé demoted himself to temporary leader, only to be named president later that same year in an election plagued by extensive tampering.

When it comes to North Korea, dynastic succession has been the number one rule for choosing state heads. In December 2011, Kim Jong-un came to power after his father died. Jong-un was third in the line of Kim dictators, following his grandfather, Kim Il Sung, and his father, Kim Jong Il.

Then there are the classic absolute monarchies: King Mswati III of Swaziland inherited the throne from King Sobhuz II; Sultan Hassanal Bolkiah of Brunei followed his father, Omar Ali Saifuddien; and King Abdullah II of Jordan took the throne when his father, King Hussein, died in 1999.

Sheikh Khalifa bin Zayed bin Sultan Al Nahyan inherited the job of both president and emir of the United Arab Emirates when his father, Zayed bin Sultan Al Nahyan, died in 2004. Six other emirates are also absolute monarchies whose sitting emirs have inherited their positions.

Of course, the line of inheritance does not always pass from father to son. In Saudi Arabia, King Abdullah assumed the throne from his half-brother, King Fahd, who in turn took over from another half-brother, all within the impressive sibling tribe produced by Saudi Arabia's founder, King Abdul-Aziz.

Of course, if your father is not a dictator, inheriting power becomes rather problematic, but the possibility cannot be entirely ruled out. In this case, the easiest way for a dictator hopeful to proceed is to marry a dictator's heir. Once that heir comes to power, it simply becomes a matter of ridding yourself of the individual in question, possibly by relegating him or her to the sidelines.

In order to approach your target, you must pay careful attention to where dictator heirs congregate. They can often be found at luxurious vacation spots, such as the French Riviera, Monaco, or some island in the Caribbean. Mingling with playboy princes and party princesses in vacation paradises is a much more pleasurable way to the top. At this point, it's all about knowing whom to set your sights on.

Of course, that is not always easy. A dictator can always quarrel with his children and find a new favorite successor. In North Korea, for example, Kim Jong-nam was long considered Kim Jong Il's chosen successor—that is, before his father changed his mind. Among the reasons for this change was the fact that the dictator's son wanted to go to Disneyland, which, unfortunately, does not have a North Korean branch. Nonetheless, Kim Jong-nam did not let his dream die. In May 2001, Jong-nam was arrested at the Tokyo airport with a false Dominican passport under the alias Pan Xiong—"Fat Bear" in Chinese. With him were two women and his four-year-old son. Jong-nam sat in holding for several days before he was sent back to China. During the interview, he said he came to Japan to visit Tokyo Disney. According to Jong-nam, he fell out with his father because he wanted economic reforms and was then branded a capitalist. He now lives in Macau, where he is known as a party animal and gambler.

Unfortunately, when it comes to inheritance, things don't always go according to a dictator's plan. In Egypt, it seemed that President Hosni Mubarak was grooming his son, Gamal, to assume power. When Mubarak was toppled in February 2011, Gamal's political career came to an abrupt halt.

Generally speaking, it is a good rule of thumb to target heirs in established monarchies. Clear rules tend to govern dynastic inheritance, and this ensures a measure of security. If one wants a good tip, there is much to indicate that Teodorin Nguema Obiang, the dictator's son from Equatorial Guinea, is being groomed to assume power from his father, Teodor Nguema Obiang Mbasogo. At present, Teodorin lives a happy jet-setting lifestyle, complete with partying, fast cars, and beautiful women.

One can also put their money on Dariga Nazarbayeva, the daughter of Kazakhstan's president Nursultan Nazarbayev. Nazarbayeva sits in the Kazakh parliament and has been named a possible heir to her father. She was divorced in 2007 and is now on the market. Her position as Crown Princess has become a little shakier in the last few years, given that she has challenged her father politically on a number of occasions. Similarly, Gulnara Karimova was long regarded by many as a potential heir apparent to her father, Uzbekistan's president Islam Karimov. In late 2013, Karimova's relationship to her father began to deteriorate, apparently because she began single-handedly conducting business without first informing him of her intentions. She was placed under house arrest, and since then, little has been heard of her—indeed, in November 2016, two months after her father died of a stroke, there were rumors of her own death by poisoning. The lesson here is to pay careful attention to what goes on in the dictator's court. You do not want to risk being stuck with some disinherited dictator's spawn who has fallen out of their progenitor's good graces.

In short, there are many roads to power. The most important thing is to find out which method best suits the country you have chosen for your absolute rule. However, even after you have established yourself as dictator, your task is far from over. Coming to power is easy—remaining at the top is much more difficult.

2

HOW TO STAY IN POWER

IN 1992, SIERRA LEONE WAS governed by General Major Joseph Saidi Momoh. Momoh came to power in 1985 via an election in which he was the only candidate. Sierra Leone is a small and extremely impoverished nation, and the economic situation did not improve under President Momoh. In 1991, the war in neighboring Liberia spread to Sierra Leone, and an eleven-year-long civil war broke out.

In April 1992, the young Captain Valentine Strasser was sent to lead a company in the diamond-rich region of Kenema. Heretofore, Strasser's greatest life success had been on the dance floor, as the winner of a number of disco competitions. Without knowing it, though, he had greater things in store. Government soldiers at the time were struggling to subdue the brutal rebels active in the Kenema area, but sadly, President Momoh had forgotten one of dictatorship's most important rules: pay your soldiers.

In Kenema, Strasser was met by soldiers complaining that they hadn't received a paycheck in three months. The young and ambitious officer decided to take matters into his own hands. Informing the soldiers that he was going to solve the problem, he hopped into a car and drove back to the capital of Freetown. While he was en route, the rumor spread that he was going to the capital to topple President Momoh. When he reached Momoh's headquarters, the dictator was unprepared for such a confrontation, and Momoh immediately surrendered power—according to this version of the story, at least. Other people claim that Strasser, along with a small group of young officers, plotted to remove Momoh and they all drove to the presidential palace together that night. Once there, they discovered Momoh in the bathroom dressed only in a bathrobe. No matter which version of the story is correct, the fact remains that Momoh surrendered without a fight and quickly found himself in a helicopter on the way to neighboring Guinea.

Twenty-five-year-old Strasser then took over and became the youngest head of state to not inherit the position. Together with a junta of young officers, he governed Sierra Leone until 1996, when he was removed by a fresh military coup led by one of his own companions. Like his predecessor, Strasser was quickly shipped off to Guinea, and once again the only title he could claim was King of Disco.

Of course, Strasser's road to power was far simpler and shorter than for most dictators, but his was not the only coup in history that happened as a result of coincidence. If you find yourself in the right place at the right time, becoming a dictator does not need to be difficult. Strasser's story illustrates another point as well: the problem is not always coming to power. Staying in power over a long period of time requires cleverness, finesse, and tact—all characteristics that Strasser clearly did not possess.

VANISHING OPPOSITION

A dictator lives dangerously. It is a job that creates heavy resentment and will earn you plenty of enemies. There is a perpetual risk of coups, revolutions, and assassination attempts. In addition, you must be constantly prepared for popular uprisings, international criticism, and calls for democratic reforms. Luckily, there are ways to deal with all of this. Experience shows that an effective security apparatus, a well-thought-out propaganda approach, and elegant political maneuvering can ensure you a lifelong tenure. In some cases, it can extend your term even beyond that. Kim Il Sung, who died in 1994, is North Korea's Eternal President.

The fact of the matter is that even the best despots meet resistance on their home turf. How much opposition a dictator allows will vary, but often it will not take much to get the snowball rolling, at which point resistance becomes unstoppable. Luckily, there are a number of tried-and-true measures for limiting and stopping political opposition in its tracks.

The informant society, perfected by the Stasi in East Germany, is one effective approach. A population that lives in perpetual fear of arrest equals a docile population. Terrorizing your opponents, of course, is a classic dictator technique for keeping average people away from opposition. The easiest method for doing that is simply to weed opposition from the face of the earth. For example, in Latin America's dictatorships, it was so common for the authorities to remove people that "disappear" became a transitive verb. People talked about "disappearing someone." Jorge Rafael Videla, dictator of Argentina from 1976 to 1981, admitted in 2012 that his regime had "disappeared" between seven and eight thousand people. Killing them was necessary, claims the aging ex-dictator, who now sits in prison for murder and torture. His mistake, he contends, was letting the killings appear to be mystical disappearances.

"Let's say there were seven or eight thousand people who had to die to win the war against subversion. There was no other alternative. We were in agreement that it was the price that must be paid to win the war against subversion and we needed that it not be obvious so society would not realize it. For that reason, so as not to provoke protests inside and outside the country, the decision was reached that these people should be disappeared," Videla said in an interview with author Ceferino Reato.

The ex-dictator also admitted that children were stolen from leftist opposition families and adopted out. Let us hope their new adoptive parents ensured the kidnapped children a healthy extreme right and military upbringing.

Fortunately, there are also less violent methods for maintaining power. If you are wealthy enough, you can simply buy yourself support. Sheikh Hamid bin Khalifa Al Thani, the emir of Qatar, keeps his population content by ensuring an unusually high standard of living. The average income among the oil-rich emirate's 250,000 inhabitants is well over $50,000–60,000 a year.

HOW TO WIN AN ELECTION

Like other heads of state, dictators experience resistance and opposition from certain portions of the populace. However, in contrast to a democracy, a dictatorship offers numerous tools for keeping a leader in power, no matter what the people may think.

In a modern dictatorship, the opposition will normally demand a democratic election. In addition, you, as dictator, will be subject to international pressure to inaugurate democratic reforms. The extent of this pressure will vary. Oftentimes, it will be so light you can simply ignore it. If your country happens to be rich in oil, all objections to your authoritarian mode of government will be limited to mutterings in the United Nations' corridors. Saudi Arabia, for example, may have an authoritarian and oppressive regime, but it escapes international criticism because the world is dependent on Arabian oil. In Zimbabwe, on the other hand, there is not a drop of oil to be found. Therefore, international pressure on President Robert Mugabe to instigate democratic reforms is high.

Democratic elections are extraneous in a dictatorship. As dictator, your tenure in office does not actually depend on the will of the people. The people hardly know what is best for them anyway—that is your responsibility. Nonetheless, in some cases a "democratic" election can be advantageous, if for no other reason than to shut the mouths of irritating leaders from such idealistic micro-countries as Norway, for example. Plus, democratic elections also serve a number of other useful functions.

By allowing a small amount of opposition, you gain easy oversight regarding said opponents. Holding an election also demonstrates the goodwill to initiate democratic reforms, something you can subsequently throw in your critics' faces. And if you do things right and achieve the desired result without too much effort, an election will only strengthen your claim to legitimacy.

Fortunately, there are many ways to ensure your victory at the polls. Filling the box with your own ballots remains a popular method. The problem is that it's easily detectable. Photos and video clips taken with mobile phones can spread like lightning among voters, leading to protests both inside and outside the country. "Ballot-box stuffing" can work in isolated cases, but the trend is now moving toward other, not so obvious methods.

Thorough preparation prior to election day ensures that you will avoid anything that could awaken suspicion. Remember: you are the one making the rules, and you can arrange things so that the election's outcome will never be in doubt.

Media control is one of the most powerful tools at your disposal. Ensure that you have complete jurisdiction over the country's major television channels. Airwave monopolization is not difficult to achieve and is the norm in a dictatorship. See to it that state channels are filled with your supporters and define licensing conditions to ensure that independent channels can be immediately shut down if they become too critical and that troublesome media outlets can easily be disarmed with bureaucratic technicalities. Laws prohibiting insults to the country or the president are also good to have in your pocket when it comes to shutting critics' mouths. However, you should also make a show of granting your opposition limited media presence. This makes the illusion of a free election slightly more realistic.

Image is also important. Obviously, the media should focus on your political victories, show that the government is spending money on worthy goals, and highlight the crucial role you play in international forums. For some people, the tough-guy image has worked. A good example is Russia's strongman Vladimir Putin, whose image has been carefully constructed around the "Athletic Outdoorsman." Putin has posed on tiger hunts, fishing trips, and while shirtless on horseback. Your actual athletic prowess does not matter—the important thing is to know how to cash in on a good photo op.

Otherwise, you should play the statesman. You should appear on television duly carrying out your tasks as the nation's leader prior to actively participating in the election campaign. Of course, you can leave the actual campaigning to the media, who will flatter you and ridicule your opponent. When the media is in your hand, it is a simple matter to throw dirt on the opposition. For example, do they have contacts with other countries? Why, then they are obviously operating under the auspices of countries with imperialistic agendas.

You can also easily influence the election by making voter registration difficult for the opposition's supporters. In contrast, people who depend on your leadership and goodwill, such as soldiers, prison inmates, government employees, and employees of government-owned concerns, are more likely than other portions of the populace to vote for you. Therefore, you should ensure that these people are registered in droves—automatically through their workplace, if possible. Companies can also help influence the election by busing their employees to polling stations.

In areas where you enjoy little support, ensure that polling stations open late and close early. Long lines are a disincentive for voters. Polling stations should have too few ballots and inadequate voter lists, irregularities that can easily be chalked up to human error. Buying votes in poorer areas with free food and alcohol also tends to work well.

Another classic technique is harassing and arresting the opposition. However, like ballot-box stuffing, this method can quickly lead to protests. Of course, in a country like North Korea, where the government's grip on the populace is so firm that few dare to protest, this method works splendidly. A common alternative to violence is to stop opposing politicians at the root by making the process of declaring one's candidacy so complicated that it is always possible to end an opponent's candidacy due to a technicality.

One tempting strategy for controlling the opposition is to sponsor or engender it yourself. After receiving criticism for smothering any opposition, Kazakhstan's president Nursultan Nazarbayev allowed his own daughter, Dariga Nazarbayeva, to found the opposition party, Asar, which means "all together." She was elected to parliament in 2004. For a time, Nazarbayeva also headed the media group Khabar (in which she has an undisclosed stake), which happens to largely focus on government-friendly parties during an election. Before the election in 2004, Asar received around half of all Khabar's election coverage, and unsurprisingly, Asar later joined the president's party, Otan.

Another example is Turkmenistan's February 2012 election. A number of candidates put themselves up for election. However, they all happened to come from the party of the sitting president, Gurbanguly Berdymukhamedov. At candidate forums, all of his rivals praised Berdymukhamedov, and none of them encouraged the voters to cast ballots for themselves. Naturally, Berdymukhamedov won a crushing victory with 97 percent of the votes.

According to Joseph Stalin's secretary, the Soviet dictator put it like this: "You know, comrades, that I think in regard to this: I consider it completely unimportant who in the party will vote, or how; but what is extraordinarily important is this—who will count the votes, and how." As usual, the old communist had a point. An enormous amount can be done after the votes are collected. Ensure election boxes are left standing overnight in poorly watched offices, and let fate take its course.

Unfortunately, it is increasingly difficult to keep international election observers out. The UN and other intergovernmental organizations actively work to ensure that elections are observed in authoritarian countries. However, that is not necessarily a matter of concern. You can muster a network that guarantees you receive favorable observers from countries that would be interested in not having their own election tampering made public. These countries might be other dictatorships or countries interested in maintaining a good relationship with the dictator up for "election." It can also be advantageous to have observers from two or more organizations. Dissent among observers, which is actually quite common, tends to weaken credibility. Observers from the Commonwealth of Independent States, a club for former Soviet states with headquarters in Belarus, are more likely to ratify dubious voting procedures than, for example, UN observers are.

A skilled dictator can decide for himself just how much support he'll receive in an election. Oftentimes, it is simply a question of attaining a reasonable result. Ninety-nine percent is relatively common. Both Raúl and Fidel Castro received around 99 percent of the votes among their constituency in Cuba's 2008 parliamentary election. North Korea's deceased dictator, Kim Jong Il, received 99.9 percent in his district in the country's 2009 parliamentary election. (Voter turnout was around 99.98 percent.) Saddam Hussein holds the record, with the whopping 100 percent voter support he received during a popular election in October 2002, where he asked the people's permission to serve another seven years. Although no one has achieved over 100 percent in a general election, some dictators have certainly accomplished the impossible in individual districts. During Russia's presidential election in March 2012, aspiring dictator Vladimir Putin received 1,482 votes in District 451 of Chechnya's capital, Gorznyj. His closest rival, Communist Party leader Gennady A. Zyuganov, received only one vote. Given that District 451 only had 1,389 registered voters, Putin actually received 107 percent of the votes. Impressive!

The burning question, of course, is just how much support a dictator ought to have. If the victory is too great, it can lead to protests; if it is too low, it can provide impetus to the opposition. A victory of over 90 percent will always appear suspicious. However, some dictators have difficulty understanding exactly what their critics want. Belarus's president, Aleksandr Lukasjenko, has complained about how difficult it is to appease Western politicians. During the 2006 presidential election, Lukasjenko officially received 93.5 percent of the votes. After accusations from the West of election fraud, the dictator changed the result to 86 percent, something he readily admits. As he told Ukrainian journalists after the election: "Yes, we falsified the last election. I have already told this to the Westerners."

The president was clearly disappointed that his Western critics still would not accept the result. The Belarus dictator announced in frustration: "In fact, 93.5 percent were for President Lukasjenko. People say this is not a European result, so we changed it to 86 percent. . . . The Europeans told us before the election that if there were 'European' figures in the election, they would recognize our election. And we tried to make European figures."

START WITH THE CHILDREN

"You can fool all the people some of the time, and some of the people all the time, but you cannot fool all the people all the time," said Abraham Lincoln supposedly. Obviously, he was no dictator. Most despots spend a lot of time and energy telling the populace just how fantastic the country is under their reign.

Propaganda is one of the most important tools a dictator has. The fact that dictators almost always have a propaganda department in one form or another, something one seldom encounters in democracies, is a sign of just how critical it is for a dictator to control the flow of information. Propaganda can take many forms. Many countries showcase huge placards with appeals to the people or dictatorial words of wisdom. Textbooks are adapted so that the correct sides of the regime come to light and the dictator's accomplishments receive adequate coverage.

In an Iraqi elementary school textbook from the Saddam Hussein era, Amal and Hassan are reoccurring figures, much like the American Dick and Jane. At one point, Amal holds a portrait of Hussein and says: "Come, Hassan, let us chant for the homeland and use our pens to write, 'Our beloved Saddam.'" Hassan answers: "I came, Amal. I came in a hurry to chant, 'Oh, Saddam, our courageous president, we are all soldiers defending the borders for you, carrying weapons and marching to success.'"

At school, every subject was full of Hussein's propaganda. In gym class, students exercised while shouting: "Bush, Bush, listen clearly: we all love Saddam." In math, students were assigned problems such as: "If you shoot down four American planes holding three persons each, how many Americans have you killed?"

And when things do not go as you expected, you can always bluff. Are your crops too small? No problem! Print in the newspapers that it was a record year. Are you facing criticism from the UN? Play applause for Iraq whenever television channels show clips from sessions of the General Assembly. In a dictatorship, truth is never absolute.

At the beginning of the 1930s, Romania's president, Nicolae Ceauşescu, ordered nearly all the country's agricultural products to be exported in order to cover the enormous foreign debt he had incurred. When that created a food shortage and people starved, he dismissed the fact by stating that Romanians eat too much anyway. In order to support this assertion, he invented his own scientific diet. Conveniently, the diet was almost completely free of meat and dairy products, of which there happened to be a shortage. Ceauşescu also participated in a propaganda film in which he inspected large quantities of meat and fresh fruit in order to show that production goals had been achieved. Few knew the foodstuffs were largely artificial props.

PUREBRED RACIAL THEORY

One of the most effective ways to drive propaganda is to incite the populace against an external foe while simultaneously appealing to basic nationalistic and racist instincts. No one has accomplished this as thoroughly and successfully as North Korea's three generations of Kim. Since Kim Il Sung came to power in 1945, the authorities in Pyongyang have propagated one of the most imaginative twists on reality the world has ever seen.

The truly brilliant aspect of North Korean propaganda is the way in which different narratives are presented to different audiences. North Koreans receive one version, while foreigners are served another. Ever so slyly, Pyongyang skews internal propaganda for foreign eyes in order to prevent the world from knowing exactly what form of propaganda the North Korean population is receiving. And North Koreans receive their own version of how North Korea is perceived by the outside world. Confused? You are not alone. For more than sixty years, North Korean propaganda experts have been wrapping Americans, Russians, and the rest of the world around their little fingers.

Japan laid the groundwork. Korea became a Japanese protectorate in 1905, and Japan annexed the Korean peninsula in 1910. Prior to that, Koreans had regarded themselves as champions of Chinese culture, but now the Japanese instituted an enormous propaganda program designed to "Japanize" the Koreans. As it turns out, both peoples belonged to a morally superior, imperial race. The Koreans, accordingly, were allowed to cultivate their own brand of nationalism, just as long as it supported the narrative that they were part of a Japanese unity.

In August 1945, Soviet troops drove the Japanese out of the Korean peninsula and set up headquarters in Pyongyang. American troops arrived in September and took control of the southern half of the peninsula. Stalin, predictably enough, was not interested in allowing areas liberated during World War II to remain in peace. The Russians needed a suitable leader, and for lack of anything better, they settled on Kim Il Sung.

The thirty-three-year-old Kim Il Sung made his public debut on October 14, 1945, during a mass demonstration to cheer the Soviet liberators. Kim had spent the years of World War II in the Soviet Union but had earlier fought against the

Japanese in Mao Zedong's army. An attack on a Japanese military camp in 1937 gave him status as a guerrilla fighter.

Since no one in North Korea knew much about Marxism, the new regime began producing its own propaganda, which had a completely different flavor from that being churned out in European communist countries. Much was taken from Japanese occupation propaganda. Mount Paektu, the highest peak in North Korea, for example, fulfills the same central function in North Korean propaganda as sacred Mount Fuji does in Japanese mythology.

Koreans, furthermore, are a unique race. They are born virtuous and have an inborn purity. Therefore, they are also vulnerable. They are like children who must be protected from a vicious world. North Korean propaganda literature is full of naive and childlike Koreans, while the heroes tend to be protective mother figures. According to the propaganda, Korea is the people's natural habitat, a scenic, safe, and maternally sheltering landscape. Old fairy tales become historic fact, and according to the official narrative, Korea is rooted in Asia's oldest nation. Throughout centuries, greedy foreigners have been trying to get their grubby paws on the peace-loving Koreans' natural wealth.

In this new Korean history, Kim Il Sung became a heroic guerrilla soldier who fought the occupying power from a secret base on Mount Paektu. The fact that he actually spent the war years in the Soviet Union is beside the point.

In August 1948, South Korea declared itself independent, and North Korea followed suit a short time later. Simultaneously, Kim Il Sung made plans for a military reunion. The propaganda now featured stories of the brutal American occupation and how fervently the South Koreans would embrace the North as liberators. When the United States entered the war, it bombed North Korea. Americans were portrayed as a degenerate, backwards, and inherently evil race. A short story entitled "Jackals" showcases the way American missionaries murder Korean children by giving them a shot of deadly bacteria. This short story, regarded as nonfiction, is still extremely popular in North Korea.

Of course, in reality the Korean War was started by North Korea, and it was North Korea that asked to negotiate when things started going poorly. Yet, according North Korea's official history, the United States had resorted to a cowardly ambush to start the war. The peace treaty, signed on July 27, 1953, is characterized as an enemy surrender.

North Korea also played a double game with the Soviet Union, its most important ally. On one hand, in order to receive support, Kim had to appear as the ally and partner of the Communist Bloc, whereas internal propaganda continued to drive home Korean superiority. In a 1955 speech, Kim Il Sung proclaimed that "to love the Soviet Union is to love Korea" while simultaneously banning Soviet theater from North Korea. Eastern European diplomats have described hostility to foreigners by North Korean officials, not to mention the way children on the street threw stones at them.

North Korea is also crime-free, if one is to believe the country's media, which never reports local offenses. The virtuous and moral Koreans, it seems, are simply incapable of wrongdoing, although they can be seduced by malicious foreigners to carry out childish pranks. The regime also does not invent criminal complaints against its political prisoners, as is typical in other dictatorships. Instead, bothersome people simply have a way of ceasing to exist.

North Korean propaganda's one shortcoming was that it lacked an academic, revolutionary element. In a speech in December 1955, Kim used the word *juche*—meaning "subject"—for the first time to refer to the idea that the subject of ideological studies was the Korean Revolution. In the West, the speech was interpreted as an expression of Korean nationalism, something Kim duly noted. In the 1960s, Juche theory was marketed as Kim's stunning intellectual contribution to Marxist theory. If you believe North Korean propaganda, study groups all over the world are sitting down to immerse themselves in Kim Il Sung's and Kim Jong Il's texts on Juche. Since Kim Il Sung has never stood out as a particularly great ideological thinker, a backstory had to be created that would anchor Juche thought. The official history is that eighteen-year-old Kim Il Sung first voiced his brilliant Juche theory in 1930, at a meeting among revolutionaries. In 1997, a new calendar was introduced that featured Kim Il Sung's birth year, 1912, as Juche 1, and the following year as Juche 2, Juche 3, and so on. The year 2017 is Juche 106.

The advantage to Juche is that it is such a vague theory that it actually says very little. According to Kim Il Sung, the basic Juche idea is that "man is the master of all things and the decisive factor in everything." The most important Juche principles are that Korea must remain politically autonomous, economically self-sufficient, and militarily independent. Of course, Pyongyang has itself never lived up to these Juche ideals. Over the years, North Korea has received support from the Soviet Union, China, and the United States. Nonetheless, Juche fulfills two functions: first, it consolidates Kim Il Sung's position as a great political thinker, and second, it draws foreign attention away from the actual content of North Korean propaganda with its racist and nationalistic paranoia.

An external foe tends to mobilize the populace, which is something North Korean leaders have duly exploited. Anti-Americanism is a common feature of communist propaganda, but few have succeeded in painting such a nightmarish picture of the Americans as North Korea. The degenerate Americans will forever remain the enemy of all Koreans, for Americans are born evil and are beyond redemption. "Just as a jackal cannot become a lamb, imperialists cannot change their rapacious nature." So it goes. In pictures, Americans are drawn with long, hooked noses and sunken eyes. After World War II, these fiends greedily seized South Korea, whose people now suffer under terrible conditions while they dream of reuniting with North Korea under its fantastic leadership.

However, it is not just Americans who appear in the propaganda. All races are inferior to the Koreans. Friendly lands are represented as humble vassal states. North Korea, for its part, is an invincible superpower that triumphs on all fronts. When the United States and North Korea meet to negotiate, it is always synonymous with complete American surrender. And yet, even though it is an invincible superpower, North Korea is also the victim of American aggression. For outsiders, this might seem like an irreconcilable contradiction, but for the propaganda geniuses of Pyongyang it is no problem.

In recent years, however, it has become more difficult to keep the borders closed. During the famine of the 1990s, thousands of North Koreans fled to China. Those who returned brought with them stories of higher living standards. News from South Korea is also accessible to many people, and DVDs of South Korean soap operas stream across the border. These soap operas have become so popular that, according to a *New*

York Times article, state TV conducts campaigns against South Korean hairstyles, clothing, and slang.

This makes it more difficult to maintain the propaganda, of course, but not impossible. Luckily, South Korean media is also thoroughly anti-American. At the same time, it has become more problematic to assert that North Korea is more prosperous than its southern neighbor. Therefore the regime has admitted that, while South Korea is better off materially, it still longs for the freedom and racial purity enjoyed by the North. Southern prosperity is entirely due to the United States' attempt to transform the colony into a showcase.

In June 2011, North Korean TV news presented a global happiness index. According to the index, North Korea astonishingly ranks as the second happiest nation in the world. China heads the list with one hundred of one hundred possible points. North Korea, for its part, received ninety-eight points. Third on the list was Cuba (ninety-three points), which was followed by Iran (eighty-eight points) and Venezuela (eighty-five points). South Korea achieved a measly 152nd place with only eighteen happiness points, while the US is naturally the world's most miserable country. That the Chinese people appeared happier than the North Koreans on the index can only be due to the fact that it's not possible to keep their neighbor's greater prosperity a secret.

The practical response to this in North Korean propaganda is that it does not promise the population material goods. While Marxism-Leninism, which North Korea embraces in theory, suggests that people become more prosperous over time, North Korean leaders can always argue that external threats force the country to prioritize defense over their people's standard of living. The leader's most important job, after all, is protecting the pure Korean race, even if that requires material sacrifice. North Korea's lack of prosperity is explained by the fact that the military requires all necessary resources.

Directed internally, state propaganda features Koreans as a superior race that must be shielded from the rest of the world, but externally, such racism is not mentioned. To the outside world, North Korea represents itself as a Marxist state, with Juche as its local ideological approach. Foreigners are also tricked into thinking that internal propaganda describes North Korea as a communist paradise. What are North Koreans told about the country's relationship to the rest of the world? That foreigners are awestruck by North Korea's development, and they study Juche theory for dear life in order to catch up. Despite this, because we are all members of inferior races, there is no reason to treat us with respect. When meeting with foreign colleagues, North Korean leaders and diplomats are almost always described as arrogant and patronizing, as befits a master race.

The North Korean regime demonstrates how a well-oiled propaganda machine can keep a dictator in power despite difficult bumps in the road. If you cannot fool people all of the time, you can certainly fool many over the long term.

3

CULTIVATE YOURSELF

ONE OF THE MOST FASCINATING things about a dictatorship is the way in which a dictator comes to permeate all aspects of society. This is not merely due to the statues and portraits adorning public places and offices, though such public art does contribute to the sense of dictatorial omnipresence. A clever dictator is also able to get beneath his subjects' skin, beneath the very surface of the landscape, and penetrate his country's every last nook and cranny.

Without this omnipresence, a successful dictatorship will be almost impossible to perpetuate over time. If you are not a god in the people's eyes, the populace can begin to question your infallibility. You cannot allow that. You must create the conception that you are integral to your people's well-being. People must set an equal sign between you and the state: without you, there is no state.

Building a personality cult is not something a dictator does just for fun or because power has gone to their head (although occasionally it does contribute). Obviously, playing God is great fun, but a successful personality cult also has a practical side. First, it creates fear: the feeling that you are everywhere makes political dissenters think twice before planning a rebellion. Second, it gives a feeling of invincibility: the threshold for challenging your sovereignty will be higher if people believe you have divine status. Third, it gives you an unlimited right to govern: challenging your leadership is like challenging the natural order.

A personality cult is also somewhat unavoidable. "Power tends to corrupt, and absolute power corrupts absolutely," wrote John Dalberg-Acton in 1887. A dictator who has tasted power will ultimately begin to believe his own propaganda.

In this section, we will visit a number of points that come into play when dictators set out to create the world in their own image—and then we will examine how the whole can be orchestrated in practice.

1. Flood the Place with Statues and Portraits

Rule number one is visibility. Erect statues of yourself in all public places, traffic circles, sports arenas—in short, anywhere people tend to congregate. Your portrait must also hang in every public office, be it a hospital or a post office, so that visitors can see who is in charge. Many dictators are lazy about updating their portraits, and decades-old portraits will accordingly adorn the walls of public offices. However, some dictators consider it crucial that their image stay current. When Turkmenistan's deceased dictator, Saparmurat Niyazov, dyed his gray hair black, all public portraits had to be exchanged or retouched. Painters were dispatched overnight to update the large presidential images adorning buildings in the capital. According to official propaganda, Niyazov's black hair was proof of his good health.

2. Give Yourself a Title

A title or epithet sounds good and distinguishes you from more run-of-the-mill state leaders. Your title should contain some association with statesmanship, courage, paternalism, and love. Naming yourself after animals also works well. Mobutu, long-time dictator of the Republic of Zaire, assumed the impressive nickname Mobutu Sese Seko Kuku Ngbendu waza Banga, which means "the all-powerful warrior who, because of his endurance and inflexible will to triumph, proceeds from conquest to conquest, leaving fire in his wake." His parents gave him the humbler name of Joseph-Désiré Mobutu. The African dictator was also called "The Leopard."

3. Erect a State Philosophy—Give It a Snappy Name

"Religion is the opiate of the masses," wrote Karl Marx. If anything will keep your subjects in check, it is opium. Unfortunately, it is rather difficult to keep a country's entire populace in a perpetual opium daze. Marx also teaches us that we can replace opium with a mindset. It does not have to be religion per se; just something that resembles religion, such as a state ideology. State ideologies function wonderfully as substitute religions. Just look at what the Soviet Union did with Marxism! Every self-respecting dictator further shapes a national ideology with a religious character. Make sure that you occupy a central place in the official mythology.

Muammar Gadhafi's ideology also had a snappy title: "The Third International Theory," which is a combination of Islam, Libyan tribal traditions, socialism, and pan-Arabian nationalism. We'll take a closer look at Gadhafi's political theories in chapter seven.

4. Write a Book

People need access to your political thoughts. Therefore, you should write them down. Of course, most politicians can produce classic political nonfiction. Your written works, however, should have a visionary character, offer moral guidelines, and be nation-building. Literature is a well-proven method of propagating one's message. A small, easily transportable book is not a bad idea. Just look at Mao Zedong's little red collection of proverbs.

5. Make Sure That the News Is Always about You

State media exists for a single purpose: to tell the world all about you and your activities. Make sure that newspapers, TV channels, and radio stations cover every aspect of your official enterprises. No news item is too small, so long as it doesn't contain anything negative about you.

6. Name Everything after Yourself

As the country's most important person, it is natural for important buildings and sites to bear your inscription. It is also most typical to name streets after yourself. Every city of a certain size should have at least one street bearing your name. Schools, hospitals, and universities should be named after whoever is financing them. Airports are another favorite. Let your name be the first thing incoming travelers meet and the last thing they see before they depart. Those who really embrace the concept of grandeur will name cities after themselves, like Rafael Trujillo, who changed the capital of the Dominican Republic from Santo Domingo to Ciudad Trujillo. Trujillo, who liked to spread it thick, also changed the name of the country's highest mountain from Pico Duarte to Pico Trujillo.

7. Pass Quirky Laws

Some dictators forget this point, especially considering how much fun it is to have an entire populace dancing to your strings. It might seem counterproductive to ban drumming on weekdays, as Jean-Bédel Bokassa did in the Central African Republic. Still, this kind of law shows people just how personal your power is. You really are the one in charge.

THE SUN KING

In 1990, Saparmurat Niyazov became Foreman of the Supreme Soviet—the highest position of authority in the Turkmenistan Soviet Republic. When the USSR collapsed a year later, the Supreme Soviet declared Turkmenistan an independent state with Niyazov as president. In June 1992, Niyazov won the young nation's first presidential election in a crushing victory. He was the sole candidate.

Niyazov quickly began building a state ideology with himself front and center. He assumed the title of Turkmenbashi, which means "Father of all Turkmen," and is often extended to Beyik Turkmenbashi, "Turkmenbashi the Great." Placards posted around the country sported the slogan "Halk Vatan Turkmenbashi"—The People, the Motherland, Turkmenbashi—summarizing the Holy Trinity that was Turkmenistan's essence.

At first glance, Turkmenistan hardly seems worth the trouble of building a dictatorship. After all, only 5 percent of the country's land is arable, and the rest is desert. The majority of the population, which numbers around five million, lives below the poverty line. However, Turkmenistan sits atop one of the world's largest gas reserves, and few things give a dictator as much leeway as do oil and gas. Furthermore, the country is strategically situated, sharing borders with geopolitical hotspots Iran and Afghanistan.

Eventually, Turkmenbashi created one of the most extensive and eccentric personality cults the world has ever seen. He was a master of naming things after himself. Of course, a number of streets were given the name Turkmenbashi, and when you arrive in Ashgabat by plane, you land at the Saparmurat Turkmenbashi International Airport. The city of Krasnovodsk on the Caspian Sea was also renamed Turkmenbashi, and there are several vodka brands that feature the president's picture on the label. For people wanting to smell like the president, a Turkmenbashi perfume was produced. Niyazov did not stop there. On June 20, 1998, a meteorite landed in Turkmenistan and was promptly dubbed Turkmenbashi. A mountain peak was honored with the president's name.

Niyazov also proceeded to rename the months. Naturally, the first month of the year became Turkmenbashi. April was named after his mother, Gurbansoltan. May was named for Turkmenistan's national poet, Magtymguly, and September was called Ruhnama, in honor of a book Turkmenbashi published. The dictator seemed especially interested in honoring his mother. The word for bread was changed from *chorek* to "Gurbansoltan Edzhe," his mother's full name. Weekdays also received new names: Monday became *bashgun* (main day), Tuesday *yashgun* (young day), Wednesday *hoshgun* (happy day), and Thursday *sogapgun* (justice day). Friday went from *anna* to *annagun* (which still means "Friday"), Saturday became *rukhgun* (spiritual day), and Sunday, *dynsjgun* (rest day).

Like any good dictator, Turkmenbashi introduced a number of quirky new laws. Long hair and beards were outlawed, and heedless travelers were given a shave and a haircut at the border. When Niyazov stopped smoking in 1997, he banned smoking in all public places. Gold teeth, an extremely popular replacement for bad teeth in many former Soviet republics, were outlawed too.

Turkmenbashi banned ballet, opera, and circuses. Singers were forbidden to lip-synch to recorded music. Female news anchors could no longer wear makeup. The reason: Turkmen women were more attractive without artificial aids, and the dictator failed to see the difference between women and men when the women appeared with makeup.

Of course, presidential statues popped up everywhere. The crowning glory was a triple-footed, 246-foot-high tower outside the presidential palace in the capital of Ashgabat. The tower, dubbed the Arch of Neutrality, was topped by a thirty-foot-tall, gold-plated statue of Turkmenbashi. The statue rotated so that the dictator's face was always turned toward the sun.

Turkmenbashi's literary masterpiece, *Ruhnama*, became Turkmenistan's new Bible. The book is a blessed (in the word's literal sense) blend of autobiography, spiritual guidance, and history. The country's mosques were required to place the book next to the Koran. The presidential staff weighed the possibility of elevating Turkmenbashi to an Islamic prophet but didn't want to agitate Muslims outside the country.

In short, Niyazov followed the recipe for a personality cult to the letter. He flooded the country with statues and portraits of himself, took a title, introduced a national, semi-religious philosophy with his book *Ruhnama*, saturated the media with his presence, named everything possible after himself, and passed a heap of quirky laws. Indeed, Turkmenbashi's personality cult took on a scope that people believed impossible in most countries outside North Korea. It was therefore a sad day when Turkmenbashi died on December 21, 2006. Thankfully, his successor, Gurbanguly Berdymukhamedov, has done his best to fill his predecessor's shoes.

When one dictator succeeds another, he has two possibilities for creating his own personality cult: he can build on his predecessor's cult, or he can depart from it and start from scratch. An example of the former is North Korea's leaders. Berdymukhamedov, for his part, opted for the latter. Having previously served as minister of health in Niyazov's regime, he could hardly condemn his predecessor's government, but he could eliminate Turkmenbashi's omnipresent fingerprint and replace it with his own. Shortly after assuming power, Berdymukhamedov began removing Turkmenbashi's statues and portraits. Months and days reverted to their original names. A test on *Ruhnama* was no longer a requirement for entering the university, and in 2013, the book was removed from the school curriculum.

Other than that, Turkmenistan's new dictator laid low for a few years. He published some books on Turkmen horses and native medicinal plants, but otherwise, there was little resemblance to his predecessor's visionary building projects and grandiose self-image. In 2011, however, things started to pick up speed. The country's media began referring to the president as "Arkadag," meaning "Protector." Later on, the title was formally awarded to him by Turkmenistan's Council of Elders.

Turkmenistan's dictators also have a special penchant for naming their time in office. Naturally, these titles reflect the president's unparalleled leadership skills. Turkmenbashi governed the nation through the Epoch of the Great Renaissance, and later, through Turkmenistan's Altyn Asyr, or Golden Age. For his part, Arkadag dubbed his first presidential term the Epoch of Great Rebirth. In February 2012, things were going so well in Turkmenistan that the media declared the country to be headed for an Epoch of Might and Happiness.

Berdymukhamedov has continued Niyazov's tradition of naming things after family members. A rural school in the Akhal province is now named after the president's grandfather, Berdimukhammed Annaev. In contrast to the majority of other schools in the country, this one is equipped with modern technology. The president's father, Myalikguly Berdymukhamedov, was a policeman, and the unit in which he served now bears his name. His father's office has been restored and turned into a museum.

It was several years before Berdymukhamedov began erecting statues of himself. The first was unveiled in March 2012. The president was portrayed in white marble on horseback. Obviously, Berdymukhamedov likes horses. Aside from writing the aforementioned book on Turkmen horses, he has introduced a holiday celebrating Turkmenistan's national horse race, Akhal-Teke.

The president also displays great artistic talent. Following a television appearance where he played the guitar and sang his own composition, "My White Rose for You," his guitar was declared a national treasure and sent to a museum.

PAPA VOODOO

Though they certainly are candidates for "Best in Class," Niyazov and Berdymukhamedov are not the only dictators to succeed in building up a comprehensive personality cult. One of the more interesting dictators in this category is François "Papa Doc" Duvalier, who governed Haiti from 1957 until his death in 1971.

Duvalier was born in 1907, during a time when the country was governed by a mulatto elite while the black populace largely lived in poverty. The young Duvalier studied medicine at the University of Haiti and later community medicine at the University of Michigan. In 1943, he worked for an American company that was trying to prevent the spread of a number of tropical diseases, including typhus and malaria. Gratified patients began calling him Papa Doc, a nickname he would keep the rest of his life.

Eventually, Papa Doc became involved in Haiti's Négritude movement, which fought against racial oppression. He was also attracted to the Haitian Voodoo religion, and his Voodoo skills would serve him well when he later became dictator.

In the 1940s, Duvalier served as minister of public health and labor in the Haitian government but was forced underground following a coup by General Paul Magloire in 1949. Magloire left the country after a series of strikes and protests in 1956. In 1957, Duvalier declared himself a candidate in the presidential election. His political message was to decry that the mulatto elite was becoming rich at the expense of the black majority. As the military's preferred candidate, Duvalier had a certain advantage. The first election results came from Gonâve Island outside of Port-au-Prince. Duvalier received 18,841 votes, while his opponent, Louis Déjoie, only 463. That is quite an impressive result. According to a 1950 census, Gonâve only had 13,302 inhabitants. In total, Duvalier received 678,860 votes to Déjoie's 264,830.

It was not long before Papa Doc began to pursue his opponents. He formed a paramilitary police force, the Tonton Macoutes, who murdered and tortured the opposition and collected informal taxes. The force was named after the mythical figure Tonton Macoute, who stuffed bad children in a gunny sack and ate them for breakfast. The members did their best to live up to the name—they would decapitate their victims and leave the bodies in the markets as objects of terror and warning.

Duvalier made certain that the population was made fully aware of his Voodoo skills. When he talked, he stared out into the air while whispering words and moving very slowly, a sign that a person is in contact with the spirits. He invited Voodoo priests to the presidential palace and planted rumors of his supernatural adventures. "My enemies cannot get me. I am already an immaterial being," he said in a speech. He also claimed that John F. Kennedy's assassination in 1963 happened because he had cursed the American president.

In 1959, Duvalier suffered a heart attack. Clément Barbot, the head of the Tonton Macoutes, acted as Duvalier's substitute while the dictator was recovering. When Papa Doc returned, he suspected Barbot of wanting to take power and imprisoned him. When Barbot was freed in 1963, he began working against the president. When the Tonton Macoutes discovered Barbot's headquarters, they peppered it with bullets. After the soldiers had finished shooting, they kicked in the door to the house. Out walked a black dog. The house was empty of people, but Barbot's weapon stash was present. When Duvalier discovered that Barbot had transformed into a black dog, he decided that all Haiti's black dogs must be destroyed. Barbot was eventually discovered in human form by the Tonton Macoutes and shot shortly thereafter.

Throughout the 1960s, small guerrilla units consisting of Haitian exiles attempted to seize the country. After a guerrilla soldier was killed, Duvalier ordered him to be decapitated and the head brought to the presidential palace on an ice block. It was said that Duvalier used his supernatural abilities to interrogate the head for hours to recover information on the insurgents' plans.

On June 14, 1964, Duvalier arranged a national referendum for a new constitution that declared him President for Life, granted him absolute power, and gave him the right to choose his successor. The voters could choose between blue, pink, yellow, and red ballots, though they all held the same word: "Yes." Everyone, including foreigners, was ordered to vote.

By 11:15 a.m. on the morning of the election, Duvalier gave a speech in which he proclaimed: "Today the people have expressed their will. I believe that, as I am now speaking to you, I am already President for Life of the republic." In the speech, he also addressed himself in third person, a not uncommon trait among dictators, and was surprisingly honest about his intentions in becoming President for Life: "He is a suspicious man. He will govern like a ruler. He will govern like a true autocrat. I repeat: He accepts no one else before him."

The next morning the votes were tallied: 2,800,000 votes for the new constitution, with 3,324 people voting against it, even though it is unclear how anyone could have succeeded in voting no.

In 1966, Duvalier convinced the Vatican to give him the right to appoint priests in Haiti's Catholic Church, thereby assuming control over the country's two largest religions, Voodoo and Catholicism. A famous propaganda picture shows Jesus standing upright behind a seated Duvalier, with the phrase "I have chosen him."

The Lord's Prayer was rewritten in praise of Duvalier, who was naturally mightier than God. The new text ran: "Our Doc, who art in the National Palace for life, hallowed be thy name for present and future generations. Thy will be done in Port-au-Prince as it is in the provinces. Give us this day our new Haiti and forgive not the trespasses of those anti-patriotic intruders who daily spit on our land. Lead them into temptation, and beneath the weight of their poison, free them not from evil."

A pamphlet distributed after Duvalier was elected President for Life proclaimed the following:

"Question: Who are Dessalines, Toussaint, Christophe, Petion and Estimé?

Answer: Dessalines, Toussaint, Christophe, Petion and Estimé are five distinct Chiefs of State who are substantiated in and form only one and the same president in the person of François Duvalier."

Dessalines, Toussaint, Christophe, and Petion are heroes from the eighteenth-century Haitian Revolution, and Dumarsais Estimé was president while Papa Doc served in the government during the 1940s.

Naturally, this new catechism was taught in all the country's schools.

Papa Doc also changed the Haitian flag from red and blue to red and black, which happen to be the colors that symbolize Voodoo. Anthropologist Wade Davis succeeded in infiltrating the secret Bizango society, the most important secret Voodoo society in Haiti. He discovered that the chief divinity the Voodoo congregation worshipped was Duvalier himself. Altars in the secret Voodoo temples were dominated by pictures of the president. Rituals required black virgins, pierced hearts, rum flasks, swords, and spades to dig graves.

When Papa Doc died in 1971, his nineteen-year-old son, Jean-Claude Duvalier, took over as president. The young dictator was naturally given the name Baby Doc. Shortly after coming to power, Baby Doc had placards hung all over Haiti proclaiming the following: "I should like to stand before the tribunal of history as the person who irreversibly founded Democracy in Haiti." The placards were signed "Jean-Claude Duvalier, President for Life."

Sadly, the young dictator was wrong. In contrast to his father, Baby Doc did not serve as president for life. In 1986, he was forced to step down and flee to France in exile after the populace rose against him.

Papa Doc was far from the only dictator with supernatural abilities. President Teodoro Obiang Nguema Mbasogo of Equatorial Guinea was described by the national radio station in 2003 as being like "God in heaven," who has "power over all men and things." "He can kill without anyone holding him accountable and without going to hell because it is God himself, with whom he is in permanent contact, who gives him strength," proclaimed one of the president's staff on the radio program *Bidze-Nduan* (*Bury the Fire*).

Gambia's president, Yahya Jammeh, claims that he can cure AIDS, a gift he received in a dream. Jammeh regularly treats HIV-positive patients. For the duration of their treatment, patients must abstain from alcohol, tobacco, tea, coffee, theft, and sex. It is unclear why theft is specifically cited, but one can assume it means that other crimes do not influence the regimen. Patients receive traditional plant medicine and are advised to discontinue Western medications, such as antivirals, while the president's treatment progresses.

Unfortunately, Jammeh has no intention of revealing exactly what ingredients make up the medicine or of allowing his patients to be independently tested. "I don't have to convince anyone. I can cure AIDS and I don't want to explain it to those who don't want to understand," Jammeh declared to the television channel Sky News.

Jammeh can also make childless women fertile and cure asthma, and his supernatural abilities do not stop there. He claims that he possesses amulets that protect him against weapons.

"No knife or bullet shot from a gun can kill me without the will of my Lord," he apparently told Gambian journalists.

THE DYNASTY

North Korea's leaders have woven the world's most comprehensive state mythology on nation, folk, and leaders. The country's unique propaganda myths naturally include an extensive personality cult. As mentioned in the preceding chapter, Koreans are the purest, most virtuous, and most moral race. However, they are not exactly the strongest, and their propaganda doesn't emphasize intelligence either. Consequently, Koreans throughout history have been exploited and vanquished by inferior races. In order to survive and maintain their unique characteristics, Koreans require a strong leader who can protect them.

This propaganda fits hand in glove with the personality cult that has been built around the country's founder, Kim Il

Sung. As it turns out, Kim Il Sung was the most naive, loving, spontaneous, and pure Korean—the most Korean of all the Koreans—ever born.

Given that, the basic problem facing the North Korean propaganda machine was how to combine the image of Kim Il Sung the guerrilla hero and strong leader with the innate Korean virtues, which don't suggest that Koreans are great fighters. The mythology doesn't actually explain this contradiction, but the aggressive sides of the war's history are toned down. Even though he was represented as a military genius, the propaganda's primary focus was on Kim Il Sung's concern for his soldiers and not the battles themselves. The leader was shown with his troops while they ate or rested, but seldom in battle.

While heads of state in other dictatorships are consistently described as their nations' fathers, the feminine side of the North Korean leaders is emphasized. For instance, Turkmenistan's Saparmurat Niyazov's title of Turkmenbashi promotes him as Father of Turkmen. Another dictator who was declared to be his nation's father was Joseph Stalin. François Duvalier's nickname of "Papa Doc" is yet another example. Even though the nickname was given before Duvalier became president, he had no qualms about using it after he came to power. In North Korea, on the other hand, the leaders are often described as mother, rather than father, figures. In propaganda pictures, Kim Il Sung is represented as plump and childlike, usually surrounded by enthusiastic children throwing their arms about him. He is a kind of androgynous—or hermaphroditic—person, who is often referred to by the gender-neutral word parent.

Following the Korean War, the public mythology surrounding the Great Leader focused on his tireless voyages around the country. The leader would arrive at a factory or farming collective and be presented with a problem, about which he held on-site counseling sessions. His advice was usually simple and quotidian. On one occasion, his wise words were as follows: "Rainbow trout is a good fish, tasty and nutritious."

Kim obviously took inspiration from Chairman Mao Zedong. Since Mao led his troops through the Long March, Kim could hardly do any less. He established a Korean counterpart, the Hard March, on which he supposedly led his guerrilla soldiers during the winter of 1938–39. Since Mao was recognized as a poet and author, an opera that Kim Il Sung wrote in his youth suddenly came to light.

Although Kim Il Sung died in 1994, he is still the Eternal President of North Korea. In order to emphasize how integral Kim was to Korean well-being and underpin the official rhetoric, North Korea endured some hard years after the leader's death.

Kim Jong Il, Kim Il Sung's oldest son, assumed leadership of the country. The personality cult was in place to prepare the people for a Dear Leader, a title Kim Jong Il had already received by the 1980s (or rather, "Dear Ruler," since in Korean the title "Leader" is reserved for Kim Il Sung). Kim Jong Il was said to have been born on the sacred Mount Paektu during the war (actually he was born in the Soviet Union), and was said to be a self-sacrificing and patient little boy who never received special treatment, despite the fact that he was the son of the country's Great Leader. Instead, Kim Jong Il was represented as a child who suffered much, having lived through two wars and lost his mother when he was small.

At the same time, Kim Jong Il was represented as a military leader to a greater extent than his father. In 1991, he became commander-in-chief of the country's troops. He launched the political slogan "Military First" in 1995. This slogan implies that the country's defense is so important that the military is prioritized at the expense of economic development in other areas of society.

Propaganda couldn't conceal the fact that times were worsening, although the 1990s hunger catastrophe (i.e., the catastrophic famine) in North Korea was not Kim Jong Il's fault. It was blamed on the Soviet Union's cowardly surrender to capitalism, multiple natural catastrophes happening around the world, and the United States' increased attempts to crush North Korea after Kim Il Sung's death. The difficult years of the 1990s were described as a new Hard March in order to revive memories of the fictive Hard March that had been used to cement Kim Il Sung's personality cult. Kim Jong Il visited military bases across the country, and in sympathy with his soldiers, he ate the same simple rations as they did. In contrast to his father, Kim Jong Il never appeared publicly in suits but instead appeared in an informal and flattering uniform, in order to underscore the Dear Leader's simple needs.

Kim Jong Il occupied the same androgynous parent role as his father. His position as leader for the "Military First" political approach didn't prevent the mythology from representing him as motherly, something the following extract from the state news bureau Korea Central News Agency demonstrates:

> Held together not by a mere bond between a leader and his warriors, but by the family tie between a mother and her children, who share the same blood and breath, Korea will prosper forever. Let the imperialist enemies come at us with their

nuclear weapons, for there is no power on earth that can defeat our strength and love and the power of our belief.

Our Great Mother, General Kim Jong Il!

With Kim Jung-un, the propaganda machine took a new direction. Kim Jong Il's second son by his third wife became North Korea's new leader after his father died in December 2011. Even before the young Kim came to power, his image had been built up in order to prepare North Koreans for their coming dictator. On October 10, 2010, the sixty-fifth birthday of the Workers' Party of Korea, a documentary was broadcast on North Korean television that claimed Kim Jong-un had intrinsic knowledge of politics, economy, culture, history, and military affairs. According to the program, he spoke fluent English, German, French, and Italian, and was learning Chinese, Japanese, and Russian.

A brochure distributed to farmers in the Hamgyong province describes how Kim Jung-un invented a new type of fertilizer while he was visiting a collective farm with his father in 2008. Stories also circulate about Jong-un discovering crimes while traveling incognito around the country, and that he is a fantastic shot who always hits his target (a rare hint that criminal activity takes place in North Korea).

During official appearances, he is always made up and styled so he unmistakably resembles his grandfather, Kim Il Sung. He has his grandfather's chubby form, and some commentators have speculated that he has undergone plastic surgery. It is important for the propaganda machine to strengthen associations with the country's founder, perhaps because the average North Korean had a higher standard of living under Kim Il Sung than under Kim Jong Il.

4

HOW TO GET RICH

ONE OF THE MOST IMPORTANT reasons to become a dictator is the prosperity it brings. There are many ways to secure an uninterrupted system of corruption and a perpetual cash flow, but here are some useful, basic guidelines that all despots who wish to amass a small fortune should know.

A country's resources are often identified as community goods. But what does that mean exactly? Who has the right to distribute to the populace whatever riches just happen to exist in their homeland? A dictator, for his part, regards natural resources as communal goods to a limited extent, but he also considers much of the country's wealth to be his own personal property. As dictator, it is your privilege to govern the country's natural resources and help yourself to anything you need or want.

Almost all dictators develop a widespread practice of corruption. As such, the world's most corrupt heads of state are typically dictators. In fact, in 2004, the organization Transparency International, which is dedicated to fighting corruption, compiled a list of the previous decade's most corrupt state leaders. Mohamed Suharto, who governed Indonesia from 1967 to 1998, apparently squirreled away between $15 and $35 billion. Behind him is Ferdinand Marcos of the Philippines, with $5 to $10 billion; Mobutu Sese Seko of the Republic of Zaire, with $5 billion; Sani Abacha, with $2 to $5 billion; Slobodan Milosevic, with $1 billion; and Jean-Claude "Baby Doc" Duvalier of Haiti, with $300 to $800 million. Indeed, we must scan down to seventh place in order to find a non-dictator: Peru's former president, Alberto Fujimori—and he was definitely no diehard democrat either.

Corruption has a tendency to trickle from the top on down. It seems impossible for a corrupt dictator not to create an entire system of corruption beneath him, but this is no cause for alarm. For a dictator, there are clear advantages to having a corrupt regime. People are greedy, and as long as they are assured a piece of the pie, there is a real likelihood they will remain loyal—and loyalty is not something a dictator can take for granted. There is another advantage in letting people get their hands dirty: they become accomplices.

In a corrupt state, money flows up to the top of the chain of command. As dictator, you can't waltz around demanding bribes for every little thing. You have to build a corrupt system, which starts with the lowest officials.

Nepotism is a central ingredient here. One would be hard-pressed to find a dictator who has not filled important positions with his relatives and friends. It is also not uncommon to favor people from the same religious or ethnic group. As such, one makes sure loyal people always occupy key positions.

Egypt's Hosni Mubarak, for example, ensured that his two sons, Alaa and Gamal, received fantastic opportunities in both business and politics. At the beginning of the 2000s, Gamal embarked on a political career that quickly moved him to the top of Egypt's political elite. Eventually, he became deputy secretary of the state party, NDP, and presided over the party's policies committee. Many people assumed he was being groomed to take over as president when Hosni either died or became too old.

Mubarak's sons also functioned as his contacts in the business world, and this benefited all concerned. In addition to making Mubarak a very rich man, his sons accumulated substantial fortunes themselves.

Indeed, one of Mubarak's strokes of genius was to fill his parliament with businessmen. This move produced a fusion of politics and economics that made it easier for the Egyptian dictator to conduct business. For their part, these businessmen gained advantages through political influence—advantages, by the way, on which Mubarak could expect returns. The Egyptian dictator also employed a common dictator trick for securing business opportunities: foreigners who invested in Egypt were required to have a local business partner who also owned parts of the enterprise. Unsurprisingly, Mubarak's family members turned out to be partners compatible with many investors.

Once you have filled key positions with your own people, you can start to stuff your pocketbook. One important tool is regulation: you must regulate every last detail of society. When it comes to conducting business with ease, dictatorships usually rank lowest on the scale, because the strictest possible regulation and control paves the way for the greatest amount of corruption. For example, it is common in dictatorships to require businesses to have licenses. Be sure to make the bureaucratic procedures involved so laborious and time-consuming that no one will bother to follow them. Instead, to secure a license, one simply bribes a functionary.

This practice (and the associated corruption) can be doubled by also introducing strict controls on the import of key raw goods. For instance, if a person wants to open a bakery, he must first pay to receive his baker's license and then pay again for a license to import wheat.

Obviously, as dictator, one should strive for the least possible transparency. Budgets and accounting should be treated like state secrets, and the media should be kept utterly in the dark. (Then again, the media should already be under such strict control that no request for insight is made.) It is especially important to keep a lid on agreements surrounding the exploitation of natural resources. As a rule, these agreements are made between large international corporations and local governments.

Equatorial Guinea, for example, is famous for concealing the details of the country's oil deals. Foreign firms are responsible for the actual oil recovery, and the amount of money Equatorial Guinea receives from production is a well-kept secret. As such, no one knows just how much the country's dictator, Teodoro Obiang Nguema Mbasogo, is skimming off the pot.

Secret agreements like these benefit the oil companies. Concessions undoubtedly come cheaper if the companies agree to keep the price for them under wraps. Of course, it can be rather troublesome to deal with idealistic organizations that fight corruption, but so long as foreign oil companies are allowed to join the fun, there is little danger that their native countries will demand extensive changes.

Case in point: Equatorial Guinea's dictator probably needn't worry about interference from his more democratically oriented partners. In a 2009 letter from the US ambassador to Equatorial Guinea, published by WikiLeaks, the sender recommends that

President Barack Obama keep the regime in Malabo stable. If it is not, American oil companies will lose contracts and American jobs will be lost. (The American companies Marathon Oil Corporation and Hess Corporation have enormous sums invested in Equatorial Guinea, and 20 percent of America's oil imports originate from there.) In fact, according to the WikiLeaks document, the outlook for a continuing positive relationship between the US and Equatorial Guinea is quite favorable. Equatorial Guinea has more people with the surname Obama than anywhere else in the world. As the letter states: "The recent change in the US administration—in the country with the highest per capita density of 'Obamas' in the world—was received as a herald of warmer relations."

Of course, not all dictators are swimming in luxury. For example, Zimbabwe's president, Robert Mugabe, leads a frugal life, and so did Ayatollah Ruhollah Khomeini of Iran. Iran's spiritual leader occupied a small apartment in Shahid Hassangaten on the outskirts of Tehran. When he died, all he left was a prayer rug, a small book collection, simple furniture, and a radio. For Khomeini, economic status was subordinate to religion and morals both in private life and in politics. "Economics is for donkeys," he was quoted as saying.

The Ayatollah's successors, however, are not equally frugal, certainly not when it comes to Khomeini. Just after the Ayatollah's death in 1989, construction began on Khomeini's mausoleum. The complex, which is still under construction, will include a tourist center, a theological university, a shopping center, and parking for twenty thousand cars. Altogether, the facility covers more than eight square miles. Khomeini must be writhing in his sarcophagus at this extravagance, which is located beneath a golden dome supported by thick marble columns.

Apparently, dictators who come to power for ideological reasons are less inclined to enrich themselves. Khomeini led a revolution against Shah Mohammad Reza Pahlavi's brutal government in Iran, while Mugabe was one of the leaders in the guerrilla war against Rhodesia's white apartheid regime. However, Mugabe and Khomeini are the exceptions. Most dictators succumb to the temptation to stuff their pockets, no matter what their original intentions might have been.

A country's dictator may choose the frugal life, but that does not mean the elite will follow suit. As a general rule, a dictator has plenty of relatives, tribesmen, clansmen, or others who expect a slice of the pie. There will always be people who see the economic advantage in being part of the power structure. For a state head, loyalty among staff and allies comes at a price, and therefore, living a frugal lifestyle is seldom synonymous with a low private consumption rate.

Zimbabwe is a good example. A number of members of Mugabe's circle have used their positions to amass enormous wealth. Mugabe's wife, Grace, is famous. Her lifestyle has earned her the nicknames Dis Grace, Gucci Grace, and the First Shopper. Leo Mugabe, the dictator's nephew, runs an extensive business network within the country. His company, Integrated Engineering Group, has secured a number of contracts for the construction of public buildings, often at the expense of more experienced entrepreneurs. This alone has earned him billions of dollars.

Or take the cellular operator license that was up for grabs in 1997. The license itself was distributed by Runaida Joice Mugari Mujuru, who at the time was Zimbabwe's information, post, and telecommunications minister. Mujuru, part of the old, powerful elite around Mugabe, is one of the heroes from the war of liberation and was long regarded as a possible presidential successor. Two companies were competing for the license: Telecel, in which Mujuru's husband and Leo Mugabe had ownership stakes, and Econet, operated by a businessman without a valuable governmental connection. Econet had been trying for years to build a cellular network, only to be thwarted by Mugabe, who had banned private mobile telephone companies. (This decree was later rejected by the Supreme Court, which only goes to show that even a dictator can experience bumps in the road.)

In the end, the contentious cellular license was naturally awarded to Mugabe's friends, despite the fact that Telecel's license application didn't meet all the requirements. Sadly, when it came to actual implementation, Telecel proved not especially effective and was hampered by uncertainties surrounding who actually owned the company's stock. During an ownership dispute some years later, it emerged that Leo hadn't actually paid for his stake in the company. The president's nephew emphasized the advantages of being related to the dictator when he admitted in an interview that he hadn't paid because "it wasn't necessary."

YOUR MONEY IS MY MONEY

Most dictators succeed in amassing a small fortune during their time in office. You don't need to govern a rich country—even in the poorest countries, state leaders have succeeded in squeezing the populace enough to ensure their days are spent in luxury. In

1986, the year Jean-Claude Duvalier left Haiti, the island was one of the world's poorest nations. The gross national product per person was a measly $342. Nonetheless, Duvalier and his associates had managed to squirrel away $500 million since he became President for Life in 1971. This was thanks to Duvalier having monopolized the tobacco export and pretty much every other lucrative venture in the country.

Dictators number among the world's richest people. There will always be an element of uncertainty surrounding the actual size of a dictator's wealth, of course. It is generally unclear where the dictator's private economy ends and the public economy begins. Secondly, dictators are reluctant to disclose how much they are actually worth. Transactions are made through straw firms, investments placed through fronts in tax havens, and the actual money stashed in countries where the account holders can remain anonymous.

As a dictator, the most obvious means of getting rich is to treat the state's coffers like your personal piggy bank. Unfortunately, this method does not work well in dictatorships that have a certain tradition of transparency and distinction between state institutions. For instance, in Zimbabwe, the Supreme Court has a relatively large degree of autonomy. This doesn't mean that the dictators in these countries cannot get rich at the state's expense. It is simply that accumulating wealth must happen in more subtle ways.

Absolute monarchs, on the other hand, seldom have this problem. Many of the world's richest people are monarchs, among them Queen Elizabeth of Great Britain. Before his death in 2016, King Bhumibol Adulyadej of Thailand was among this group and was in fact the world's richest monarch.

His son, crown prince Maha Vajiralongkorn Bodindradebaya-varangkun, became the tenth king of the Chakri dynasty on December 1, 2016. He will inherit the royal fortune and most likely succeed his father as the world's richest monarch too.

Of course, most contemporary monarchs wield only symbolic power, even though their royal family fortunes typically derive from eras when they were the de facto dictators. Generally speaking, monarchs who have retained their old privileges are the most well-off. With the exception of Thailand's king, absolute rulers top the list of the world's five richest monarchs. Among the twenty richest monarchs in the world, eight are dictators: the emir of Abu Dhabi, the king of Saudi Arabia, the sultan of Brunei, the emir of Qatar, the sultan of Oman, the king of Swaziland, the king of Bahrain, and the king of Jordan.

According to *Time* magazine, Sultan Hassanal Bolkiah of Brunei was the world's second richest monarch in 2015, making him the world's richest absolute monarch. The sultan is good for $20 billion.

He is closely followed by Saudi Arabia's King Abdullah bin Abdul Aziz al Saud. With a net worth of $18 billion, the king is definitely no pauper. In Saudi Arabia, the wealthy royal family controls, so to speak, everything of value. And that is no small thing. The country has the world's second largest documented oil reserves. Members of the royal family, of course, earn the most from oil production.

Number four on the *Time* list is the emir of Abu Dhabi, Sheikh Khalifa bin Zayed bin Sultan Al Nahyan. In addition to being the absolute ruler of Abu Dhabi, Sheikh Khalifa is also president of the United Arab Emirates, a federation of seven independent monarchies. Khalifa is estimated to be worth $15 billion.

The sultan of Brunei is perhaps the best example of a wealthy absolute monarch who makes no distinction between personal and public economies. The monarch who treats the state's coffers like his own personally determines how much money goes toward public welfare and how much goes toward private use. Of course, when the state and the monarchy melt into one, it is rather misleading to talk about private use. Instead, it is a matter of what portions of public funds are spent on the monarchy and what portion on his subjects. Luckily, the territories of most of the world's remaining absolute monarchies coincide with some of the world's largest oil fields, which makes the job of monarch a very lucrative profession indeed.

Brunei is a country of under 2,300 square miles, a little less than the state of Delaware, and has around 400,000 inhabitants. It is located on the north coast of the island of Borneo, and with the exception of its South China Sea coastline, the country is entirely surrounded by Malaysia. Officially, the country is called Brunei Darussalam, which means Brunei, Abode of Peace. A beautiful name for a beautiful nation. Eighty percent of the country is forested. Brunei has roots going back to the 700s, but the sultanate was established in the 1300s.

In Brunei, the sultan is called Yang di-Pertuan, which means "head of state." To underscore who the country's highest authority actually is, Bolkiah named himself both president and prime minister. Additionally, he is minister of finance and minister of defense—which makes him the supreme commander of the armed forces as well. He has also pegged himself as deputy inspector general of the police. One would think that all these positions would give him a rock-solid basis for power, but the sultan must still have feared someone would challenge his sovereignty. In 2006, he altered Brunei's constitution, thereby cementing his infallibility into law.

Like the Gulf States, Brunei is an oil country, something that has made Bolkiah one of the world's richest men. At one point, he was the richest man on earth. It is said his wealth increases by $100 a second.

One fine point about treating the state's coffers like your personal piggy bank is that you receive all the credit when the state spends money on ordinary folk. Due to its enormous oil revenue, Brunei is a welfare state (often called a Shellfare state, since Royal Dutch Shell has a large interest and wields a substantial amount of influence in the country). Education and health services are free, and there is no personal income tax. As such, the sultan ensures his people remain satisfied while his own bank account steadily expands.

CONCORDE AND PINK CHAMPAGNE

In many countries, practical limits make it impossible for the dictator to use state coffers as his own personal pocketbook. The happy melding of personal and public economies is enjoyed only by the luckiest of dictators. Although a dictator might lack total ownership of state funds, his fingers do not have to stay out of the pot. On the contrary, there are a number of other ways to empty state coffers.

One of them is a form of government known as kleptocracy, or government by thievery. Kleptocracy implies that the ruling elite occupies power exclusively to enrich themselves as much as possible. This governmental form has been practiced with great success in countries whose economy is based largely on raw-material production.

Mobutu Sese Soko of Zaire was among those dictators who developed kleptocracy to the utmost. Transparency International has estimated that he amassed a personal fortune of somewhere between $1 and $5 billion in the three decades he governed what is now the Democratic Republic of Congo. In 1985, *Forbes* magazine estimated that Mobutu had a fortune of around $5 billion, an amount equal to Zaire's foreign debt at the time.

Of course, little of this alleged fortune has been found since Mobutu was toppled shortly before his death in 1997. The British journalist Michela Wrong writes in her book, *In the Footsteps of Mr. Kurtz: Living on the Brink of Disaster in Mobutu's Congo*, that the dictator enjoyed such an expensive lifestyle that it is possible not much money was left. Whether all the money was spent or is still sitting in secret bank accounts the world over remains unclear, but one thing is certain: Mobutu and the rest of the Congolese elite were prodigious consumers.

As long as his own personal expenses were covered, Mobutu was not especially interested in economics or governmental finances. He was undoubtedly an intelligent man but had neither the patience nor discipline required for long-term political and economic planning. According to Wrong, when economic questions were discussed, Mobutu's gaze would grow distant, and his thoughts would wander. Instead, he believed in the economic miracle cures proposed by less competent advisers.

Even though Mobutu did not have the country's economics in order, he had no problem in securing himself a large portion of the revenue produced by the Congo's enormous riches.

In 1973, he introduced so-called Zairization, an effective nationalization process: Mobutu declared that foreign-owned enterprises should be handed over to the "nation's sons." The result was a race among Zaire's elite to see who could grab the most. Mobutu naturally took his share. He expropriated fourteen plantations that he then united into a large conglomerate, which together employed twenty-five thousand people, making Mobutu the country's third-largest employer and fourth-largest producer of cocoa and rubber.

Mobutu made sure he received his share of the country's enormous mineral resources as well. His method was simple. The state company responsible for marketing minerals abroad simply signed over a portion of the sale to Mobutu's foreign bank accounts. He also received money directly from producers. In 1978, an employee of the International Monetary Fund discovered that the chief of Zaire's central bank had ordered the mining company Gécamines to deposit all income from exports directly into the president's bank account. Raking in money from Congo's large diamond deposits was even simpler. Diamonds do not need to be refined and are easily smuggled out of the country. Mobutu simply needed to undervalue Zaire's diamond production, sell the diamonds on the Antwerp market, and stick the proceeds in his pocket.

When the Cold War ended, Mobutu lost Western support and needed money to keep the country afloat. During a meeting in Washington, DC, that was designed to secure the country a loan, a bank employee suggested that Mobutu could use the funds he had stashed abroad to help Zaire's people. Mobutu apparently replied: "I would like to, but my people could never pay me back."

Mobutu spent his money almost as quickly as he earned it. Pink champagne and desserts were flown in from Paris. In

Zaire, Mobutu built private villas in all of the most important cities. One of his favorite haunts was a replica of a rural Chinese pagoda in Nsele. He also spent much of his time on the luxury yacht Kamanyola, a refitted riverboat that sailed up and down the Congo River. Henry Kissinger and François Mitterrand were among the celebrity politicians invited on board.

In his home town of Gbadolite, he built a white marble castle, nicknamed the "Versailles of the Jungle," even though it was actually modeled after Laeken Palace, the official residence of the Belgian royal family. He made sure the town had an extra-long runway fit for the Concorde jets he chartered when flying to and from Europe.

Otherwise, the town's infrastructure didn't interest him much. Mobutu told Rwanda's president, Juvénal Habyarimana: "I've been in power in Zaire for thirty years, and I never built one road." He proceeded to clarify the reason roads were unnecessary: "Now they're driving down your roads to get you."

Mobutu was not content with merely owning properties in his own homeland. He purchased Villa del Mar in Roquebrune-Cap-Martin on the French Riviera (not far from the summerhouse owned by the Congo's former proprietor, King Leopold) for $5.2 million. Rumor has it that Mobutu, after the price was negotiated, asked the seller if the sum was in dollars or Belgian francs. The first sum is thirty-nine times larger than the second, but that obviously did not make much difference to Mobutu.

He bought a country house in the Swiss village of Savigny, a fashionable apartment in Paris, and Casa Agricola Solear in Portugal's Algarve for $2.3 million, a property that included 20,000 acres of land, twelve bedrooms, and a wine cellar with 12,000 bottles. A substantial portion of Mobutu's properties were in Brussels, the capital of one-time colonial power Belgium, where he owned nine buildings in the hoity-toity districts of Uccle and Rhode St. Genèse.

Kleptocracy is the most direct and obvious form of corruption, but it requires a couple of prerequisites. The first is a weak civil society. Media and other organizations must have so little influence and be so intimidated that they pose no threat to the established order. At the same time, public institutions must be so feeble that they are unwilling and unable to challenge the dictator and his allies. It helps to have an uneducated populace and widespread illiteracy. Of course, not all dictators enjoy the weak institutions Zaire had under Mobutu, but if the conditions are right, kleptocracy is a quick and proven road to economic security.

SCAMMING WITH STYLE

If the aforementioned methods don't work to earn you money, outright scamming is always a possibility—the fact that it is illegal is beside the point. As dictator, you are above the law. Of course, it is best to remain undetected, but if anyone is so bold as to snoop into your affairs, you have recourses: you can imprison the troublemakers or simply cause them to vanish. And if your grip on the media is firm enough, the danger of the news spreading is relatively small.

Kenya's Goldenberg scandal is a good example. The scam took place in the 1990s under Daniel Arap Moi, who was then president. Apparently, almost all the top politicians in Moi's government were involved.

In order to attract foreign currency, the Kenyan government passed a law entitling all exporters who deposited American dollars in Kenya's Central Bank to receive 20 percent over the exchange rate when they changed the money to Kenyan shillings. The ordinance also functioned as a form of export subsidy.

In a thoroughly corrupt country like Kenya, of course, such subsidies are invitations to scam. Businessman Kamlesh Pattni, one of the scam's key figures, founded the company Goldenberg International to export gold from Kenya. According to an agreement with the Kenyan government, Goldenberg would receive an additional 35 percent when they exchanged the income from the gold sale into Kenyan shillings. The problem is that Kenya's gold production is minimal. Therefore, the gold was smuggled in from the Congo and then transferred to Pattni, with very little—or most likely, no—gold at all actually being exported. Pattni and a number of corrupt government officials were left holding the pot.

After Moi's successor, Mwai Kibaki, came to power in 2002, he founded his own Goldenberg Commission to get to the bottom of the matter. According to the commission's witnesses, as much as sixty billion Kenyan shillings ($850 million) were stolen from Kenya's Central Bank in 1991. This number amounted to a fifth of Kenya's gross domestic product.

THINK OF THE FUTURE

Once a dictator has raked in some money, he must hide it where no one can find it. If you invest money in your homeland, you risk losing it all the day you lose power. If you are sent into exile—unfortunately, a common fate among dictators—it is essential that you have a fallback reserve.

Tunisia's dictator Zine El Abidine Ben Ali experienced firsthand the dangers inherent in keeping one's cash at home when he had to clear out of Tunisia in January 2011 after his people rebelled against him. In one palace alone, several million euros, dollars, and Tunisian dinars were discovered in a secret vault located behind a bookcase. Shelves full of boxes holding sealed envelopes from the Tunisian Central Bank were also found, in addition to valuable jewelry. Still, Ben Ali didn't leave Tunisia empty-handed. Reportedly, Ben Ali's wife Leila hit the Central Bank and grabbed one and a half tons of gold (worth $60 million) before the couple fled to Saudi Arabia.

The most obvious place for a dictator to hide his money is in a Swiss bank or in another country with weak banking regulations. It is also popular to invest in property. If you do it right, you can end up with a handsome return. It can also be rewarding to have country houses and other properties spread throughout the world. Paris, London, and the French Riviera are among favorite dictator haunts. Gold is also never a bad investment idea, as it is easily transferrable and transportable. There are also a number of other possibilities. The emir of Qatar and his family invest much of their money in art, which has led to Qatar becoming the world's largest buyer of modern art. The emir's daughter, Sheikha Al Mayassa Bint Hamad Bin Khalifa Al Thani, has been especially central in securing an enormous art collection for the Persian Gulf country. The trade in expensive artworks often occurs between middlemen, ensuring that the buyers remain anonymous. Therefore, it is impossible to know exactly how much the Qatarian dictator's family has spent, but they have bought a number of works by artists such as Roy Liechtenstein, Jeff Koons, Andy Warhol, and Damien Hirst. Mark Rothko's *White Center* set the record as the most expensive postwar painting, sold at auction when the emir and his wife bought it for $72.84 million in 2007.

As you can see, dictatorship, so to speak, is an automatic guarantor of wealth. The paths to it are limited only by your imagination.

5

HOW TO SPEND YOUR FORTUNE

IT IS ONE THING TO accumulate a fortune and quite another to spend it. Squandering money looks easy from the outside, but it takes hard work and determination to attain dictator-class luxury consumption. If you're going to burn money, learn from the masters. Few people let the good times roll with the same ease and arrogance as dictators and their families. Indeed, as dictator, you are almost required to wallow in luxury, splurge on absurd status symbols, and arrange spectacular parties and ceremonies.

When it comes to spending habits, the country's economy is no barrier. Just because the general populace lives in poverty is no reason for you not to lead a decadent and carefree life. To the contrary, as the people's chief and guiding light, it is important that you mark that difference and underscore that you, as head of state, deserve better than the average citizen.

King Mswati III of Swaziland is a good example of a dictator who swims in luxury while his people politely live a simple lifestyle. According to *Forbes*, Mswati has a fortune of $100 million and he is involved in many of Swaziland's business undertakings. Apparently that isn't enough to live on, because the king also receives a stipend from the state. In 2011, that meant 210 million emalangeni, equivalent to almost $135 million. That was about as much as the government spent on medicine, including HIV drugs, in a country where a fourth of the population is HIV positive. In 2014, the stipend was reported to be $50 million. Mswati also controls a fund of $10 billion established by his father, King Sobhuza II. The fund ostensibly exists for the good of the people, but only a fraction of the money has been spent on investments that would benefit the average citizen. More than 65 percent of Swaziland's population lives on less than $1.25 a day.

Mswati's rate of consumption is boosted by his penchant for polygamy. As of September 2013, he had fifteen wives. The typical dictator's wife often accounts for a significant portion of the family's luxury spending. A long list of shop-till-you-drop dictators' wives have burned tens of millions on shopping trips abroad, including Imelda Marcos of the Philippines and Zambia's Grace Mugabe. Compared to one measly wife, Mswati's many wives multiply the shopping fun and have been observed multiple times on shopping trips in Europe and Asia. A shopping trip in 2008, which was reported in the local press, led to demonstrations in Swaziland. The king answered by forbidding the media to report on the royal family's spending habits. (No one can say the protests didn't achieve anything!) In the summer of 2010, a good portion of Swaziland's queens, together with an entourage of more than eighty people, went to London and Brussels to shop. The previous year, at least five of the wives, together with their entourage, were seen on a shopping trip to France, Italy, Dubai, and Taiwan, where they blew through several million dollars. Neither of these trips led to protests.

There are few places where dictatorial consumption stands in such stark contrast to people's standard of living as in North Korea. In that communist paradise, all are equal, and Western consumption culture is condemned as morally reprehensible. However, the enterprising North Korean leaders nonetheless succeed in overcoming their own principles and wallowing in boundless luxury.

Not much information leaks from North Korea, and what emerges is often unsubstantiated rumor. Still, defectors have provided a few glimpses into the habits of the North Korean elite. One of them is of the former North Korean colonel, Kim Jong Ryul, who was President Kim Il Sung's personal shopper for years. In 1994, he defected to Austria after faking his own death. In 2010, two Austrian journalists published a book in which Kim Jong Ryul tells his story. His career as procurer began in 1972, when Kim Il Sung wanted a Mercedes. Kim Jong Ryul was chosen because he knew German and had engineering skills. He was sent to Vienna, where he lived for sixteen years with a diplomat's passport so that he could easily send products across the borders.

Kim Jong Ryul handled expensive carpets and gold-plated guns for the Great Leader. Kim Il Sung had a fondness for expensive foreign cars and had a number of luxury villas with crystal chandeliers, silk wallpaper, and high-end furniture.

According to the personal shopper, Kim Il Sung exclusively ate foreign food. His cooks were sent to study at famous schools in Vienna because the dictator had heard rumors that the Austrian kitchen was especially delightful—a rather amusing fact, given that Austria is seldom considered a culinary powerhouse. Perhaps Kim Il Sung simply craved Wiener schnitzel and apple strudel! Kim Il Sung's son and successor, Kim Jong

Il, was a well-known gourmand. Of course, the North Korean leaders keep their private lives hidden from both foreigners and their own people, but a Japanese man with the alias Kenji Fujimoto, who was Kim Jong Il's cook from 1988 to 2001, has cast some light on the secretive Kim family. In *Kim Jong Il's Chef*, Fujimoto tells how he traveled around the world to collect delicacies: mangoes from Thailand, seafood from Japan, caviar from Uzbekistan and Iran, oil from the Czech Republic, and pork from Denmark.

Fujimoto described Kim Jong Il as an extremely picky eater. Kitchen employees sorted through grains of rice to cull out those that were broken or deformed. Only perfect grains can be served to the Dear Leader. And there, folks, is a standard worth striving for.

THE KAISER'S NEW CLOTHES

As dictator, you should maintain a steady, high level of consumption. Therefore, on special occasions, you really need to go all out. Weddings are the perfect opportunity for you, as dictator, to show the world just what your safe holds. The wedding between Jean-Claude "Baby Doc" Duvalier and Michèle Bennett in 1980 cost $3 million. The fireworks alone amounted to $100,000.

Naturally, weddings of family members are equally important. Mobutu Sese Seko spent $3 million when his daughter Yakpwa married Belgian businessman Pierre Janssen. Two thousand five hundred guests were invited to attend and were flown in on chartered jets. Thousands of flasks of champagne were drunk, the cheapest of which cost more than one hundred dollars, the most expensive over six hundred. It cost $75,000 just to rent the plane used to fly the thirteen-foot-tall wedding cake in from Paris. Mobutu bought his daughter three wedding dresses—one for the ceremony before the mayor, one for the church, and one for the party that evening. The dresses were designed by French designers Nina Ricci, Jean Louis Scherer, and Christian Lacroix. Mobutu couldn't let the newlyweds start their new lives without a roof over their heads, so he gave them a house in Brussels, a villa in Kinshasa, and an apartment in Monte Carlo.

Jean-Bédel Bokassa of the Central African Republic was responsible for one of the dictator world's most legendary money-guzzling enterprises. Bokassa's personal consumption and grandiose building projects already stood in stark contrast to the simple lives of his subjects, but his megalomania didn't stop at material goods.

Bokassa's history is not unlike that of a number of other postcolonial African dictators: a difficult childhood, a missionary-led education, and a military career. Bokassa was born on February 22, 1921, one of Tribal Chief Mindogon Mgboundoulou's twelve children in what was then French Equatorial Africa. After having demonstrated against French colonial authorities, his father was killed. His mother was so despondent that she committed suicide.

The family sent the orphaned children to a school on a mission. There, Bokassa developed an affinity for a grammar book written by Jean Bédel, and his teachers began calling him Jean-Bédel. On May 19, 1939, Bokassa enlisted in the Free French Forces. He took part in liberating Brazzaville in the Congo from the Hitler-friendly Vichy regime in France and participated in the Allied landing in Provence in 1944. After the war, he was sent as a soldier to French Indochina, where he married a seventeen-year-old local girl.

In 1962, two years after the Central African Republic became independent, Bokassa joined the new nation's armed forces and was given the job of building the army. The following year, he was the supreme commander of five hundred soldiers and on his way to becoming the most influential person in the young nation, substantially aided by President David Dacko, who was Bokassa's cousin.

Bokassa liked to display himself in full dress uniform beside the president and did his utmost to be seen with the right people. He often argued with the chief of protocol, Jean-Paul Douate, because Bokassa had a habit of sitting in the wrong place at the president's table. Dacko received repeated warnings that the young and ambitious officer posed a threat to his power, but the president didn't take them seriously. He should have. On New Year's Eve 1965, Bokassa made his move and toppled Dacko in a quick and effective coup.

Bokassa quickly introduced a series of bizarre laws. All persons between eighteen and fifty-five years old had to prove they were employed or risk being fined or jailed. Beating the tamtam was allowed only at night and on weekends. A moral brigade was assembled to ensure appropriate conduct in the capital's bars and nightclubs.

Corruption, brutality, and random exercises of power— Bokassa largely followed the general trends for African despots at that time. However, the Central African dictator had greater ambitions than his colleagues. His French military training had made him fascinated by Napoleon Bonaparte. Since Napoleon had called himself emperor, Bokassa could do no less. On

December 4, 1977, he was crowned emperor in the capital of Bangui.

The coronation ceremony is a study in ostentatious consumption. In preparation, horsemen were sent to riding school in France to prepare for the parade that would lead the way to the actual coronation. Two hundred and forty tons of the world's most exclusive foods were flown to Bangui. The German artist Hans Linus painted two portraits of the future emperor, one with a crown and one without. A French composer created two works for the event, an imperial march and an imperial waltz, and a poet wrote a twenty-verse ode to Bokassa. One of the verses reads as follows:

> Bokassa, the new Bonaparte
> Bangui, his illustrious city
> Eclipses Rome, Athens, Sparta
> By its brilliant beauty

The total coronation cost is calculated to be $22 million, a fourth of the country's annual budget. At that point, two-thirds of the country's four million inhabitants lived on less than one dollar a day. Afraid to lose influence in the region and, in particular, access to the empire's uranium mines, France footed most of the bill, but local businesspeople were also required to chip in if they hoped to continue operating. For example, most of the diamonds used in the emperor's jewelry were gifts from the country's diamond dealers.

The ceremony was orchestrated by the French artist Jean-Pierre Dupont. The diamond-studded crown was created by goldsmith Claude Bertrand. Together with the imperial scepter, sword, and various other small things, the goldsmith's bill totaled $5 million. Bokassa's throne was made from gold-plated bronze and weighed two tons. The seat itself was placed in the belly of an enormous gold eagle and valued at $2.5 million.

Bokassa's choice of wardrobe demonstrated just how inspired he was by Napoleon. His garb was designed by Guiselin, the same firm that made the uniform for Napoleon's coronation. The emperor's coronation costume was decorated with thousands of small pearls, and he was, as befit an emperor, outfitted in a thirty-foot-long crimson mantle. The tailor's bill topped $145,000. His wife, future empress Catherine, was dressed in a $72,000 gold dress from the French fashion house Lanvin.

However, Bokassa desired more similarity to the Napoleonic ceremony than just the uniform maker. The future emperor did his best to convince Pope Paul VI to come to Bangui to crown him. The idea was to take the crown from the pope and place it on his own head, just as Napoleon had done when he was crowned. The Vatican politely responded that the pope was too old to make the trip to Central Africa. They didn't add that the pope was no longer in the business of crowning regents.

The coronation itself took place at the basketball stadium known as the Jean-Bédel Bokassa Sports Palace, which is located on Jean-Bédel Bokassa Avenue, not far from Jean-Bédel Bokassa University. During lunch, which included antelope, foie gras, and Iranian caviar, Bokassa leaned toward Robert Galley, France's minister of cooperation and the chosen representative for the occasion, and whispered: "You never noticed, but you ate human flesh." It was probably a joke, but it helped to reinforce Bokassa's reputation as a cannibal.

Of the 2,500 foreigners invited, only six hundred came. Many thought it was simply too embarrassing to participate in such a gaudy and self-glorifying event. The world's reigning monarchs were all on the invitation list, but only Prince Emmanuel of Liechtenstein showed. Not even Bokassa's contemporary African dictator colleagues Idi Amin and Mobutu participated. Bokassa later commented on the disappointing turnout: "They were jealous of me because I had an empire and they didn't." There is a good chance he was right.

Unfortunately, Bokassa's imperial career ended a short two years later, following an event that caused France to turn against its former ally. On January 18, 1979, schoolchildren and university students in Bangui demonstrated after Bokassa decreed that every schoolchild and student at Jean-Bédel Bokassa University must dress in uniform. (Coincidentally, the firm that made the uniforms was owned by one of his wives, and every uniform sported an image of Bokassa.) The military shot and killed dozens of demonstrators, but the unrest continued into the spring and finally Bokassa had had enough. The young demonstrators were arrested, and Bokassa himself participated in their abuse. Around one hundred schoolchildren died, some only eight years old. After receiving details of the massacre, France reinstated Dacko, while Bokassa fled to exile in Paris.

LIVE IN STYLE

Dictator spending often reveals a tough competitive instinct. It appears that there are certain luxury items that especially awaken fierce competition among dictators. The goal: to secure only the largest, most expensive, and most extravagant. As dictator, you should have the biggest yacht, the fastest car, the costliest jet, and the most luxurious palace around. Use and benefit of the item usually come second.

Of course, a suitable residence is essential. The bigger it is, the better, and often more than one residence is best. In addition to palaces at home, you should naturally own properties abroad. After all, you cannot be stuck in some hotel when on a Paris or Rome shopping spree. It is also useful to have a place in reserve, just in case, God forbid, you are forced into exile.

When it comes to architecture and interior design, dictators tend to have similar tastes. Sumptuous, flashy, and sparkling are key words. "Less is more" has no meaning; rather, "more is even more" is the mantra. Despite the grandeur, however, there also tends to be a pervasive femininity. An omnipotent dictator is so secure in his masculinity that he is not ashamed of pastel colors and sparkling jewels. What follows are the main characteristics of dictatorial interior design.

Think Big

This almost goes without saying. The bigger your palace, the more power you broadcast to the outside world. No matter where they're located, presidential palaces and kingly castles tend to be large. Dictators, though, have a tendency to exceed all others. The sultan of Brunei has the largest and probably the most luxurious presidential palace in the world. This architectural masterpiece, which covers over two million square feet, is called Istana Nurul Iman, which means "palace of the light of faith." The palace has 1,788 rooms and, among other things, 257 baths, a banquet hall that holds up to 5,000 people, and a mosque with space for 1,500 people. The garage can hold 110 cars, a fraction of the Sultan's collection. The palace was built in 1984 and cost $400 million.

It should be added that Brunei's government and its administration also occupy the palace and take up some of that space. However, should the sultan require a little distance or some time away from his daily tasks as head of state, he has three other palaces. Not small ones either.

Think Retro

Dictators favor forward-thinking, modern architecture for their public buildings, but when it comes to their own residences, they tend to be more conservative. Many find inspiration in old aristocratic architecture, sometimes from their own homeland but just as often from Europe—perhaps a little surprising, as Europe currently hosts relatively few dictators. Nonetheless, many of today's dictatorships were former European colonies whose upper classes were either European or native people who emulated European fashions and mindsets.

Think Baroque

Not baroque as in the historical period (although that is not out of the question), but baroque as in excess. Minimalism is not a concept dictators understand. Modesty? Absolutely not. If you have money, let it show. Flaunt it. There is always room for an extra chandelier, you cannot have too many colonnades, and few objects are not improved by adding a stroke of gold paint.

Think Gold

Gold never goes out of style in the dictator world. It has been a favorite with despots since the Egyptian pharaohs. Most things are gold-platable. Statues and busts of yourself are perhaps the most obvious choices, but your imagination is the only limit. In addition to having a gold-plated throne, Emperor Bokassa slept in a gold-plated bed. The Cuban dictator Fulgencio Batista received a gold-plated telephone in gratitude from the American phone company ITT. Batista kindly ensured that rates in Cuba stayed up, thereby securing high profits for the company. The fact that despots have a fondness for gold-plated cranes on their boats indicates that gold symbolizes purity in the dictator world. In the bathroom of every dictator from Nicolae Ceaușescu to Ferdinand Marcos, you can wash yourself with water streaming from golden pipes.

Gold-plated weapons are also a recurring theme. Muammar Gadhafi was brandishing a gold pistol when he was captured, and various other glittering weapons were found in his palaces. Saddam Hussein had a collection of gilded guns, including multiple gold-plated Kalashnikov rifles, among others. Hussein also had a number of gold dinner plates, which ended up in the New York restaurant Park Avenue Autumn after the American invasion.

Think Selfish

You are the most important person in the world, and there is only one way to show it. Most dictators fill public spaces with their own likeness, and it is just as natural to fill your home with it. Pack your house with paintings, photographs, busts, and statues of yourself. Choose famous artists to do your portraits.

DICTATOR TRANSPORT

When dictators cannot be found in their palaces, chances are good they are aboard a gigantic yacht. Six of the world's ten largest yachts are in the hands of dictators. Sheikh Khalifa bin Zayed bin Sultan Al Nayan, president of the United Arab Emirates and the emir of Abu Dhabi, set a new world record when he built the 590-foot-long yacht *Azzam* in 2013. According to rumors, *Azzam* has fifty suites, six bridges, and a nearly six-thousand-square-foot lounge, complete with all imaginable (and unimaginable) luxury. The French interior designer Christophe Leoni is responsible for the decor, which is apparently done in turn-of-the-century Imperial style. The yacht reaches the respectable top speed of 31.5 knots.

Other Arabian heads of state are not much worse off. The emir of Dubai has a 531-foot yacht; the sultan of Oman, a 509-foot yacht; and the king of Saudi Arabia, a 482-foot yacht.

Muammar Gadhafi's son, Hannibal, in contrast, did not consider a traditional yacht to be quite large enough. The dictator's party-going son often needed a large boat on short notice for when he spontaneously decided to invite his friends to social events. Therefore, he ordered his own cruise ship to be built. Obviously, it should lack none of the traditional luxury and dictator bling, but Hannibal had something extra special planned to entertain his guests. The ship's centerpiece would be a tank with enough room for two sand tiger sharks, two white sharks, and two black-tipped reef sharks. The tank would be surrounded by marble columns, gilt-framed mirrors, and statues. In order to care for the dictator son's pets, four biologists would be employed around the clock.

The cruise ship, with room for 3,500 guests, would have been christened *Phoenicia*, but alas, it wasn't finished before Papa Gadhafi was killed and Hannibal was forced to flee the land in the summer of 2011. Of course, that gave the average Joe the chance to vacation in true dictator style. The ship was purchased by a cruise operator, renamed *MSC Preziosa*, and began sailing the Mediterranean in 2013. The shark tank was discarded, sad to say.

Other dictators also like to take to the ocean. Turkmenistan's great leader, Gurbanguly Berdymukhamedov, wanted a yacht to rival Russian billionaire Roman Abramovich's. Unfortunately, the canals leading to the Caspian Sea proved too narrow and, as Turkmenistan doesn't have a second coastline, he had to content himself with a lesser boat. This nugget of information was made public in a memo, disclosed by WikiLeaks, from the chargé d'affaires to the American ambassador in Ashgabat.

Berdymukhamedov also used his limitless power to muster a crew for the yacht. According to the classified report, seven seamen who were originally employed by the Swedish-owned shipping firm GAC were ordered to work aboard the dictator's leisure craft. One of the top heads of GAC told the ambassador that he was on vacation when office employees phoned him to say the company had received a request to borrow three employees from one their ships—a master, a chief mate, and a chief engineer. The three employees didn't want to work for the dictator, but that didn't stop Berdymukhamedov. According to the ambassador's report, "Less than three days later, his office called him again with the news that security officials were boarding the boats as they came into the harbor and taking boat documents, essentially immobilizing them."

The GAC head rushed back from Thailand to meet with the harbormaster in Turkmenbashi, who in the meantime was so grievously offended that GAC hadn't dispatched the required personnel to the president's yacht that he had turned his chair to the wall and was refusing to speak to anyone.

Once in Turkmenbashi, the GAC head finally succeeded in wheedling the harbormaster, and the three employees were transferred to the president's yacht. Turkmen authorities later demanded that GAC send four additional employees. The seamen were on temporary loan at first, but GAC was subsequently informed they wouldn't be returning to the company.

According to the WikiLeaks document, the sixty-million-euro vessel was a gift from the Russian firm Itera, which had extensive industrial projects in Turkmenistan—yet another example of the beauties of corruption.

When it comes to interior design, dictators opt for the same style on their boats as in their palaces. On the mega-yacht *Dubai*, for instance, gold, glass, and heavy wood panels dominate the decor. Naturally, the ship sports other necessities, including a helicopter pad and its very own submarine.

Of course, yachts are primarily meant for vacation and relaxation. When it comes to long trips, flying is quicker, but lines at public airports are both exhausting and time-consuming. Therefore, any self-respecting dictator has one or more private jets on hand. The sultan of Brunei has at least three enormous jets—a Boeing 767, a Boeing 747 jumbo jet, and an Airbus A340-200. The sultan naturally follows the most important interior trends on board his planes, and in true dictator style, the jumbo jet's restrooms have gold-plated sinks.

The emir of Dubai, like a number of other royals on the Arabian Peninsula, also travels by Boeing 747 when he is abroad. It was a Saudi Arabian prince who was the first to order a private Airbus A380 "Superjumbo," the world's largest passenger plane. The buyer attempted to remain anonymous but has since been identified as Prince al-Waleed bin Talal, the nephew of King Abdullah. The price tag of $488 million made the plane the world's most expensive private jet. When it was finished, the gargantuan jet had a marble Turkish bath, a concert hall with room for ten people, and a garage big enough for the prince's Rolls Royce. The private suites each have their own prayer room with electronic prayer mats that always point toward Mecca. The crowning jewel, however, is a "wellness room" with a gigantic screen on the floor showing the ground beneath, where guests can stand on "flying carpets" and watch the landscape passing below.

ARMORED LUXURY

Expensive cars are another luxury item on which dictators happily spend money. Ferrari, Bugatti, Bentley, and other producers of exclusive automobiles would certainly face a much grimmer economic situation if dictators were not steady customers.

A few brands, such as Cadillac, tend to recur frequently, not to mention the dictatorial favorite, Rolls Royce. The Soviet Union's revolutionary hero, Vladimir Lenin, apparently owned nine Rolls Royce Silver Ghosts, among other things. How that fit with the dream of a classless society remains unclear, but it could be that Lenin just had extremely grand ambitions for Russia's proletariat. In Asia, North Africa, and the Middle East, fast sports cars like Ferraris and Lamborghinis are the choice among dictators and their relatives. These cars are less popular in Africa south of the Sahara, perhaps because bad roads make the cars all but useless. Teodorin Obiang, the dictator son from Equatorial Guinea, is an exception and owns a number of supercars that fall into the multimillion-dollar category.

Mercedes is another favorite brand among dictators, and having an armored Mercedes is perhaps the primary dictator classic. Kim Jong Il was among the believers and was observed in a Mercedes 2-600 Pullman Guard armored limousine. In his book, *Escaping North Korea: Defiance and Hope in the World's Most Repressive Country*, Mike Kim writes that Kim Jong Il spent $20 million in 2001 to buy two hundred of the newest Mercedes, which he distributed as gifts to his loyal supporters.

Dictators are often in the fortunate economic situation of being able to purchase cars designed to specification. Shah Reza Khan Pahlavi of Persia was mightily impressed by Maserati's Model 3500. However, he was not content with all parts of the existing model and asked Maserati to build a new and better version. The Maserati 5000GT was born, with the first being delivered to the shah in 1959. The 5000GT is since considered by many car enthusiasts to be one of Maserati's all-time best vehicles.

Uganda's Idi Amin distinguished himself from his colleagues—he can almost be considered the dictator world's hipster—with his progressive car choice. Amin was a huge fan of the cult-favorite Citroën SM and owned a number of them. The SM was Citroën's flagship car at the beginning of the 1970s and has become a design classic.

Not surprisingly, when it comes to the amount of money spent, the sultan of Brunei far exceeds his dictator colleagues. Altogether, the royal family owns several thousand cars, while the sultan himself owns several hundred. The exact number is probably known only to the sultan. Among these are multiple examples of most modern supercars—for instance, several of the McLaren F1, dozens of Ferraris and Bentleys, in addition to a number of custom-made models. One of them is a Rolls Royce with the back end shaped like a Porsche 911. The sultan always has a Rolls Royce idling outside his palace, just in case he has to make a hasty getaway.

With over two thousand vehicles, the sultan's brother, Prince Jefri Bolkiah, has an even greater collection than the sultan. Michael Sheehan, a luxury car dealer, visited Brunei to purchase some of these cars. According to Sheehan, Jefri has eight large warehouses filled with almost everything that rates as exclusive.

Jefri served as Brunei's minister of finance from 1986 to 1997 and was responsible for the Brunei Investment Authority (BIA), which managed the country's oil revenue. After the Asian financial crisis in 1997, BIA's investments were subjected to public audit. Prince Jefri's own company, Amadeo, collapsed with a $10 billion debt in 1998. The BIA audit revealed that between 1983 and 1998 BIA had performed "special transfers" of $40 billion and that $14.8 billion had been deposited into Jefri's own accounts. As a consequence of the audit, Jefri no longer has the means to pay people to maintain his vehicles. Some were apparently sold, but most of them are simply rusting in Brunei's warm and moist climate.

Muammar Gadhafi is the only dictator who has the distinction of designing his own car. The Saroukh el-Jamahiriya (Libyan Rocket) was unveiled in 1999 on the thirtieth anniversary of the Libyan Revolution that brought Colonel Gadhafi to power. The car got its name from its pointed front end, which resembles a rocket. The goal was to design the world's safest car, and the pointed snout was adopted for safety reasons. The thought was that, in a front-end collision, the oblique nose would enable the cars to push each other aside. The catch was that both colliding vehicles had to have the same shape in order for the idea to work. The car, with room for five passengers, also had an "electronic defense system," airbags, and, in case of an accident, an automatic fuel supply shutoff to prevent fires.

"The invention of the safest car in the world is proof that the Libyan revolution is built on the happiness of man," declared Dukhali Al-Meghareff, the head of the Libyan Arab Domestic Investment Company, which was responsible for the car's development and launch. He also emphasized that the car's name proved that while others created rockets to kill, Libya designed them for peaceful and humane purposes.

It was then announced that the car would go into production in the fall of 1999, but for ten years, nothing more was heard. At a meeting of the African Union in Tripoli in 2009, an updated version of the Rocket was presented. This time the prototype was produced in Italy by the Torino-based firm Tesco TS S.p.A. The car's interior would accentuate Libyan products, such as leather, fine fabrics, and marble. In 2009, it was again announced that the car would be sent into production imminently. However, not a peep has been heard since.

6

BE SURE TO SLEEP AROUND

Among dictators past and present are people with astonishing sexual appetites. Perhaps the reason for this is simple: faced with limitless available sex, any person would be like a kid in a candy store. Or maybe dictatorship appeals to those with such enormous egos that they require constant stimulation and satisfaction. If that's true, it could be the sex drive itself that propels a person to the top of the heap. Whatever the reason, as dictator, you typically have access to all the sexual action you could desire, and the dictators before you have established precedents for how to enjoy a thriving and imaginative sex life.

A number of history's most brutal dictators have been notorious skirt chasers. Some have been particularly kinky, and as a general rule, dictators are egotistical and not terribly considerate lovers. For example, Benito Mussolini would content himself with a quickie at his desk, often without removing his clothes.

"Power is the ultimate aphrodisiac," Henry Kissinger replied when Mao Zedong asked him how a fat man like himself attracted so many women. During a Chinese summit, Mao, for his part, offered to ship ten million Chinese women back to the United States for Kissinger. "You know, China is a very poor country. We don't have much. What we have in excess is women. So if you want them we can give a few of those to you, some tens of thousands." A few minutes later he raised his offer: "Do you want our Chinese women? We can give you ten million. We have too many women. They give birth to children and our children are too many." Kissinger answered quickly and disarmingly, "That's such a new proposition, we will have to study it."

When one of Mao's advisers later pointed out that people might not appreciate the comment, Mao excused himself to his female translator, and Mao and Kissinger agreed to drop the remarks from the official minutes. The story wasn't made public until thirty-five years later.

Power is sexy, and absolute power is seemingly irresistible. Obviously, though, dictators have another advantage when it comes to attracting women: their subjects must comply. Rejecting a flirtatious despot can have fatal consequences.

If power is sexy, sex can also be a tool for power. King Ibn Saud, the founder of Saudi Arabia, united the nation by marrying women from more than thirty of the country's many tribes. He always had four wives, four concubines, and four female slaves at his beck and call. When one of the tribes spread rumors about the king's decreasing virility, he paid them a visit and took the virginity of all the tribe's young girls. He bragged that during his life he had taken the virginity of seven hundred girls.

When it comes to dictators, Adolf Hitler was among the kinkiest, and the German Nazi leader demonstrated clear masochistic tendencies. Immediately after coming to power, Hitler entered into a relationship with the beautiful nineteen-year-old movie star Renate Müller. As she told movie director Alfred

Zeisler, one night when they were together, Hitler bragged to her about how brutal the Gestapo torturers were when it came to forcing victims' confessions. After they had undressed, Hitler threw himself on the floor at Müller's feet and shouted: "I am filthy and unclean. Beat me! Beat me!" She told Zeisler that she had to do worse things, things she couldn't even bring herself to mention.

At the end of the 1920s, Hitler began a relationship with his niece, Geli Raubal, daughter of Hitler's half-sister. Otto Strasser, the brother of Gregor Strasser, one of Hitler's early allies, stated that Hitler asked Geli to undress and squat over his face. This aroused Hitler, and when he had almost reached his climax, he asked her to urinate on him. Hitler's partner of many years, Eva Braun, also hinted that Hitler had unique sexual preferences. "He only needs me for certain purposes. This is idiocy," she wrote in her diary.

Apparently, when the Russians found Hitler's remains and conducted an autopsy, they confirmed what rumor had long held: the Nazi leader had just one testicle. However, many deem Russia's claim to be pure propaganda. If it is true, it remains unclear how Hitler actually lost the testicle. Most people think it might have happened when Hitler was wounded during the Somme offensive in World War I. Another theory is that the testicle was removed to try to cure Hitler of syphilis after a prostitute infected him in his youth.

MUSSOLINI THE GIANT

The Italian fascist leader Benito Mussolini was a true Casanova. The diaries of his longtime lover, Claretta Petacci, were published in 2009 and have revealed much about his sexual preferences. Petacci became Mussolini's lover at nineteen and eventually became his preferred female companion. She called him Ben, though Mussolini referred to himself modestly as "your giant."

According to Petacci, Mussolini once told her, "There was a time when I had fourteen women and took three or four of them every evening, one after the other. That gives you an idea of my sexuality." On the other hand, according to Nicholas Farrell, who wrote a biography on Mussolini, Il Duce ("the Chief"—another fine title) had sex with at least five thousand women. "Mussolini's butler revealed that he was screwing women all the time, even behind Clara Petacci's back," Farrell said in an interview.

Mussolini's servant, Quinto Navarra, has said Il Duce had women sent to his office every afternoon until he was satisfied. The women were entered into the guestbook as "fascist guests." As a rule, Mussolini finished quickly with each of them.

BONGO'S DESIGNER PIMP

Omar Bongo, at one time one of the world's longest sitting heads of state, became president of Gabon in 1967 and governed the country for forty-two years, until his death in 2009. The diminutive dictator was called "Africa's little-big man." Bongo compensated for his short stature with platform shoes and elegant clothes and was known to be a charismatic and charming person.

He married three times and fathered more than thirty children with his wives and lovers.

However, wives and local lovers were not enough for the virile dictator. In 2004, the *New York Times* reported that Bongo had tried to seduce a Peruvian beauty pageant contestant. Peru's ministry of foreign relations claimed that twenty-two-year-old Ivette Santa Maria, a Miss Peru contestant, was invited to Gabon to host a beauty pageant.

Santa Maria said that just a few hours after landing in Gabon she was taken to the presidential palace. When Bongo appeared, he pressed a button that opened a set of mechanical sliding doors in true James Bond style. Behind them was a large bed. Santa Maria told Bongo that she was not a prostitute and had the guards drive her back to the hotel. She did not have money for the return trip and was stranded in Gabon for twelve days before someone helped her get home.

Like most dictators, Bongo valued the good life and had a special affinity for luxury clothes. He apparently spent $600,000 a year on exclusive suits, which he had flown in from France. One of his favorite Parisian designers was the Italian Francesco Smalto. Smalto had a special sales trick. Not only did he dress Bongo up, but he also helped the dictator undress—as a bonus service, the designer would send a high-end prostitute to Gabon with Bongo's clothes.

In 1995, Smalto was charged with pimping in a trial that shook the French fashion world. The charges began when police launched an investigation into the French market for high-end prostitutes, which led them to Madam Laure Moerman, who delivered "models" to fashion designers. Many of these models told police that Smalto had hired them to "carry clothes" to Bongo.

"It went very badly that evening," a woman named Monica testified. "Bongo didn't want to wear a condom and, as he had

a friend who had died of AIDS, I refused to make love to him."
A girl by the name of Chantal claimed that the price for sex
with Bongo was the equivalent of $9,000 without a condom
and $1,800 with. When the transcription of a telephone con-
versation between two prostitutes, Ariane and Sarah, was read
during the trial, the assembly gasped. "Marika telephoned me,
she had to go to Libreville. I told her that's really serious. His
friend died of the thing," said Ariane. "AIDS? That's disgust-
ing," said Sarah. "Yes, the worst is, the great couturier proposed
it," Ariane replied.

At first Smalto denied the charges, but he later admitted
that he had sent girls to Gabon because he was afraid of losing
his best client. "We noticed that a female presence facilitated
Mr. Bongo's orders," Smalto said. "I suspected that he slept
with her, but I wasn't sure."

Smalto was given a fifteen-month suspended sentence and
was fined six hundred thousand francs (almost one hundred
thousand dollars at the time). In addition, he had to pay a symbolic sum to an anti-prostitution organization. Obviously, any
dictator worth his salt could not allow himself to be pushed
around by a democracy's judicial system. Bongo recalled
Gabon's ambassador to France, and his supporters protested
the sentence outside the French embassy in Gabon's capital,
Libreville.

BUNGA BUNGA WITH COLONEL GADHAFI

Colonel Muammar Gadhafi is another dictator who has liber-
ally helped himself to female subordinates. All of his personal
bodyguards were women, which underscores this fact. The dic-

tator himself handpicked the women. All of them were virgins and, according to Tripoli's official version, all were required to take a chastity oath. Nonetheless, persistent rumors suggested Gadhafi expected sexual favors from his guards.

In an interview with the London *Sunday Times*, Gadhafi's cook, Faisal, described the dictator's sexual habits. Faisal worked for Gadhafi for seven years and was able to get a good glimpse into the Libyan leader's sex life. According to Faisal, the dictator slept with four women a day and had a prodigious demand for Viagra. Indeed, Gadhafi took so many of the tiny blue pills that one of his nurses warned him about the drug's side effects. Medications, however, were not Gadhafi's only aid: according to Faisal, another of Gadhafi's servants was sent to Paris to procure a penis extender for him. "There were four or sometimes five women each day. They had just become a habit to Gadhafi. They would go into his bedroom, he would have his way with them, and then he would come out like he had just blown his nose," Faisal said in the same *Sunday Times* interview.

Furthermore, according to the cook, Gadhafi's female bodyguards were not as virtuous as portrayed in official propaganda. "They all had sex with Gadhafi. The more canny among them became wealthy from his gifts of villas or large sums of cash," he said. Faisal also claimed that Gadhafi once had sex with four women just hours before meeting Prince Andrew of England to discuss the state of British and Libyan relations.

Former Italian prime minister Silvio Berlusconi was Gadhafi's good friend—the two heads of state had a shared interest in prostitutes, and crooked government cemented their friendship. When called for, they had each other's back—that is until

Berlusconi, sensing the changing political winds, altered course and supported the Libyan Resistance in 2011.

In 2009, Gadhafi was one vote short of being elected chairperson of the African Union. According to Nuri al-Mismari, a former Gadhafi aide who in 2010 fled to France, Berlusconi came to the rescue and sent two prostitutes to an unnamed African head of state.

"The leader was convinced and he gave his vote to Gadhafi—and from here is born the expression 'bunga bunga,' which indicates salacious, adventurous women," al-Mismari told the newspaper *Ashaeq Al-Awsat*.

"Bunga bunga" entered the Italian language in the winter of 2011. In May 2010, an underage dancer by the name of Karima El Mahroug, also known by the stage name Ruby Rubacuori ("Ruby Heartstealer"), was arrested for theft in Milan. The Milan police received a telephone call from Prime Minister Berlusconi's office during which they were told that the arrested woman was a relative of Egypt's then dictator Hosni Mubarak, something that later proved to be pure fiction.

During the investigation of the event, El Mahroug, who is originally from Morocco, declared that she'd been invited to social events held by Berlusconi. At one of the parties, she received an envelope with 7,000 euros. She claimed she was given jewelry as well but refused to have sex with the Italian prime minister. She also described Berlusconi's sex fests, the so-called "bunga bunga" parties. "Silvio told me that he had copied it from Gadhafi. It's a rite of his African harem," El Mahroug evidently told an Italian investigator.

Saadi Gadhafi, the dictator's son, enjoyed an active sex life, and not just with women—something Libyan soccer player Reda Thawargi knew a thing or two about. The men were good friends and played soccer together in the Libyan club al-Ahli. When Saadi tried to make a soccer career in Italy, he took Thawargi with him. Saadi was offered a contract with Perugia in the Italian Serie A in 2003. Unfortunately, the dictator son's talent did not match his ambitions, and he played only one match with Perugia before he was caught doping.

What the two comrades could not get from the field, they made up for in Perugia's night clubs. According to Thawargi, he and Saadi partied constantly and took girls back to their luxury hotel. Saadi also frequently brought men home. "Saadi is gay. He tried to have sex with me, but I refused. I only like girls. So, he threw me in military jail," Thawargi told the *Australian*. He was put on trial, which was quickly concluded. The judge confirmed that "if Saadi says you have done something wrong, then you must go to prison."

The soccer player sat in jail for two and a half years before he was released on February 20, 2011, when Libyans began rebelling against Gadhafi. "When the uprising began, Saadi called me to ask me to go on state television to support him because of my fame as a footballer. I refused and hid away," Thawargi told the *Australian*.

Saadi's bisexuality was also made public in a WikiLeaks report from the American ambassador to Libya in 2009. The ambassador writes that Saadi's sexual relationships with men apparently led to friction with his father. The upshot was an arranged marriage between the dictator's son and the daughter of a key figure in Gadhafi's government:

Saadi has a troubled past, including scuffles with police in Europe (especially in Italy), abuse of drugs and alcohol, excessive partying, travel abroad in contravention of his father's wishes, and profligate affairs with men and women. His bisexuality is reportedly a point of extreme contention with his father and partly prompted the decision to arrange his marriage to al-Khweildi al-Hmeidi's daughter. Creating the appearance of useful employment for Gadhafi's offspring has been an important objective for the regime.

LOVERS ON REPEAT

Perhaps Saadi just took after his father. There have been rumors that Muammar Gadhafi himself was gay, from none other than the wife of the dictator of the Philippines, Imelda Marcos. The beauty queen was sent to Libya twice, once in 1976 and again in 1977, because her husband, President Ferdinand Marcos, suspected Gadhafi was supplying the Muslim rebels in the Philippines with weapons. Imelda's task was to convince the Libyan dictator to mind his own business. When she returned with the matter unresolved, she told friends that Gadhafi was either gay or a momma's boy.

Imelda is a shining example of the power-hungry and decadent dictator wife. She is most noted for her striking beauty and enormous shoe collection, but the life of the First Lady of the Philippines was far from simple—she was forced to compete for the attention of her skirt-chasing husband.

Imelda met Ferdinand Marcos in 1953. He was immediately besotted with the former Miss Philippines contestant and began courting her. At one point, he took Imelda and two of her girlfriends to see his bank box, where he kept almost $1 million in cash. Imelda and Ferdinand were married shortly thereafter.

Ferdinand also had a lover, Carmen Ortega, who lived with him and his mother. They had been together for five years, and Carmen was often introduced as Mrs. Marcos. Ferdinand saw to it that Carmen had a new place to live, and he continued to see her after his marriage.

Many saw Ferdinand's marriage to Imelda as a political statement. Imelda came from the Romualdez family, who wielded considerable influence over the Visayan Islands. Ferdinand was planning to run for the senate, and his marriage to Imelda helped him garner votes there.

After a confrontation with Carmen, Imelda had a breakdown and was sent to New York for treatment. She had to make a choice—either leave her husband or exploit the situation as best she could. She opted for the latter.

Ferdinand Marcos was born in the village of Sarrat on Luzon Island in 1917. His family has Chinese and Japanese ancestors, and Marcos claimed descent from a fourteenth-century Chinese pirate, which may explain why he siphoned so much from state coffers. His father was a lawyer and politician who sat in the Filipino National Assembly from 1925 to 1931. Ferdinand followed in his father's footsteps and studied law. In 1946, the Philippines became independent from Spain, and Marcos was elected to Parliament in 1949. In 1965, he was chosen as president after a fierce election battle that included threats, vote buying, and fraud. Marcos represented himself as a war hero and claimed to have led a guerrilla force of nine thousand men during World War II.

In his 1968 autobiography, *Marcos of the Philippines*, Ferdinand describes his initiative as a guerrilla leader in the fight against the Japanese in World War II. There was only one problem. In reality, he hadn't fought for the Allies but against them, in collaboration with the Japanese. According to his book, Ferdinand's efforts earned him numerous medals, including the Medal of Honor from the United States, though, oddly enough, he couldn't seem to locate the medal. Luckily, he was issued a new one by the American government. Marcos was an important ally in the fight against communism, so what was one little medal between friends?

Marcos's autobiography was made into a television series, and he wanted to see it made into a movie. In his book, he had an American-Filipino lover, Evelyn, who saved his life by taking a bullet for him. A young American actress named Dovie Beams was among those interested in the role of Evelyn and, following a short meeting with Ferdinand, she became his lover and the part was hers.

With the aid of a tape recorder, Ferdinand helped Dovie rehearse her lines. When they took a sex break, Dovie let the recorder run. Soon she had a large collection of such recordings. She also swiped a good number of Ferdinand's documents when she was snuck into the presidential palace. Ferdinand too desired souvenirs of their trysts, so he took naked pictures of her with a Polaroid and at one point asked her for a lock of her pubic hair. Dovie requested a lock of his in exchange.

After a while, Ferdinand lost interest in Dovie, and the relationship fizzled. The starlet was told she was not going to star in the movie after all and returned home to the United States. It wasn't long before she showed up in the Philippines again, this time demanding money. She received $10,000 to keep her mouth shut, but she wanted $150,000. That was too much for Marcos. Dovie was abducted by the secret police and beaten. She managed to escape when they let her go to the bathroom. She called a friend in Los Angeles with influential contacts, among them California's governor, Ronald Reagan.

Dovie checked into Manila Medical Center under a pseudonym. There she received a visit from the American ambassador and consul, who brought an offer from Imelda: $100,000 to keep the affair quiet. However, Dovie believed her life was in danger. Together with the American diplomats, Dovie arranged a press conference and told the whole story. She called Marcos "Fred," so that the journalists could report the story without risk of breaking laws against criticizing the president. Dovie played one of her sex tapes, and the attendees were treated to the unmistakable sounds of sex, not to mention the Filipino dictator singing a love song they all knew to be one of his personal favorites. Copies of the recordings quickly circulated around the capital city of Manila, and student radio looped one sequence in particular, where Marcos begs Dovie to perform oral sex. The sequence ran nonstop for a week until soldiers seized control of the radio station.

American diplomats were able to get Dovie out of the country, but during a stopover in Hong Kong, there was an assassination attempt. British agents got her to safety and kept her hidden for five days. The movie was eventually finished, with Dovie Beams as Isabelle, the movie version of Ferdinand's lover Evelyn during the war. The film was titled *Maharlika* in the Philippines and *Guerrilla Strike Force* in the rest of the world, but outside of Marco's homeland it barely made a splash.

BESTIAL URGES

King Mswati III of Swaziland is part of a dying breed of absolute monarchs. The sultan of Brunei, the king of Saudi Arabia, and a handful of other Arab monarchs are the only others left.

In Europe, the closest thing is Prince Hans-Adam of Liechtenstein.

Mswati has a decent-sized harem. As this edition goes to press, there are fifteen wives, though that number regularly increases. Fifteen wives, of course, means fifteen times the chances for a scandal. Actually, the odds may be even greater than that, given that no matter how virile a king is, he probably won't be able to satisfy all his spouses.

In 2010, it emerged that Wife Number Twelve, Nothando Dube, had an affair with the country's justice minister, Mswati's good friend, Ndumiso Mamba. The two were surprised at the Royal Villas luxury hotel. Apparently, Nothando dressed in a military uniform to sneak out of the royal palace. The king's agents became suspicious and followed her, and in the hotel room they discovered Ndumiso beneath the bed.

Mamba was fired, and Dube was placed under house arrest. The king's mother, who was known as Ndlovukazi (meaning "she-elephant"), sent the traditional delegation to Mamba's village with the indictment.

In November 2011, after more than a year of house arrest, one of Dube's children was injured while playing and the queen wanted to take him to a doctor. When the guard attempted to stop her, she sprayed pepper spray into his eyes. After this episode, Dube was thrown out of the castle. Nonetheless, she is not the only queen to have grown tired of this polygamous marriage. In 2004, two other queens were involved in adulterous scandals and had to flee the country.

In Swaziland, it is a royal tradition to have numerous wives and children. King Mswati's father, Sobhuza II, had seventy wives and more than two hundred children. Mswati was born in 1968, four months before Swaziland gained independence from Great Britain. When Sobhuza died in 1982, fourteen-year-old Mswati was designated his successor. Until the prince turned eighteen, two of his father's widows each reigned for a period. In 1986, Mswati was finally crowned king. He was the world's youngest reigning monarch and had already married his first wife.

In December 2011, rumors began to circulate about King Mswati's participation in some bizarre bestial rituals. Every year Swaziland holds its annual Incwala festival. This ceremony, or "ritual of kingship," is a long tradition. It starts at the beginning of December and continues until January. The ceremony marks the king's return to official life after a period of spiritual contemplation and helps to consolidate the king's power.

The festival has always been shrouded in exaggerated mystique, but one eyewitness has chosen to speak out. Sithembiso Simelane was a member of the king's Inyatsi Regiment for ten years and participated in the festival. On his Facebook page, he gave a detailed description of what he witnessed at the ceremony, where he claims that the king was washed by a magic snake, among other things. "Now that the king has gone into seclusion, he will be stationed at Mantjolo (near Mbabane) where there is a spirit snake, known as LaMlambo, belonging to the Mnisi clan. There, he will have the snake lick him all over the body for many days. As the snake licks him, the belief is that it cleans him of all the troubles he faced this year so that he emerges a new and strong person the next year," Simelane writes. However, the true surprise is that the king must have ritual sex with an ox. During the ceremony, one bull is beaten by young men who are ritually clean until it is stunned and docile. "Mswati believes that this action signifies that his people, as they always try by all means to rise against him, will suddenly decide to abandon that action and be confused by his muti [a magical preparation]." The bull is then led to where the naked king is waiting. After the act, the king washes himself with muti on top of the carcass of the dead bull, which is later used in a feast.

The next morning a new bull is caught. This bull is not beaten senseless but is held immobile so that the king can engage in another round of bestial sodomy. This bull is spared until the next Incwala, when it is then used in the first round. After having sex with the second bull, the king cleanses himself with muti and publicly copulates with two of his wives, whose purpose is to rid him of his "demonic evils."

The royal house in Swaziland has not commented on the accusations, but during the Incwala festival in December 2011, right after the story about bestiality began to spread, the king issued a warning about so-called jealous individuals who wanted to see Swaziland's economy go downhill.

THE PLEASURE BRIGADE

Sex with animals, of course, is not a requirement if you want to be a good dictator, but Mswati's sexual habits do underscore the fact that, for despots, their imagination is the only limit. If you have less exotic tastes, you can go the way of Kim Jong Il and Kim Il Sung. They had pleasure houses erected in various parts of North Korea, where "pleasure brigades" of young women had the task of satisfying them in different ways. Some teams performed massages, others sang and danced, but the pleasure squads were also on hand for sexual pleasure. Kim Myong-chul, a prior bodyguard for Kim Jong Il, has claimed that there are around two thousand women in these groups.

Mi Hyang, who succeeded in defecting from North Korea, was recruited by a pleasure squad when she was fifteen years old. She says that the girls must be unblemished and have soft bodies. Those who are chosen receive six months' training and have to write a blood oath with their fingers. Because Kim Jong Il was so small, he did not want girls taller than five feet five inches. "When I first met Kim Jong Il, he looked so normal, like a next-door neighbor. He has many brown spots on his face. His teeth were yellowish. My previous illusion about the great leader was shattered at that very moment. But he was very considerate toward me," Mi Hyang said.

The upshot is that most dictators can count on having their needs satisfied—no matter how kinky those needs may be. After all, an entire nation stands ready to fulfill your dreams.

7

WRITE YOUR LITERARY MASTERPIECE

DICTATORS, AS A RULE, HAVE many different sides, often artistic ones. Remarkably, many of them write books. The fact that dictators write memoirs or tracts on political theory may not seem so strange—after all, many politicians do the same—but despots are also significant producers of high literature. It may be surprising that authoritarian ideology often goes hand in hand with great literary talent, but this just proves how versatile and creative you must be to succeed as an absolute ruler. In contrast to other aspiring authors, dictators hold key advantages. They don't need to bounce their manuscripts from publisher to publisher only to be met with humiliating rejections. There is little danger anyone would dare to refuse your book, and if you do encounter problems with publishers, why, you just found your own state press! As we shall see, you will have some clear market advantages as well.

A number of dictators have transformed their books into an important part of their personality cult. As a dictator, you should collect your ideological thoughts in book form and ensure that as many of your subjects read them as possible. That is not difficult. You can simply follow in the footsteps of Saparmurat Niyazov and Muammar Gadhafi and put your books in the school syllabus.

Gadhafi is one of those dictators who successfully tried his hand at literature. His collection of short stories and essays, *Escape to Hell*, is a minor classic among dictator enthusiasts. Gadhafi's literary production is full of deep philosophical insights and political thoughts. Among other things, it romanticizes traditional Libyan society and contrasts it with modern times. The book begins with two short stories where hectic city life is described as stressful and lonely, while peaceful, traditional village life is described as meaningful and beautiful.

"The city constitutes a mere worm-like (biological) living where man lives and dies meaninglessly . . . with no clear vision or insight," Gadhafi writes in "The City." Indeed, the dictator unexpectedly emerges as environmentally friendly when he describes how cities displace arable land and spit out smoke and pollution. He also exhibits contempt for urban athletic activities.

How hard the city is! And how insipid it should be to its helpless inhabitants, whom it compels to accept unreasonable things, to forcibly swallow them, and to digest them as if they were natural and reasonable. There is no better proof of that than the insignificant interests, which the city imposes on the inhabitants. One may see crowds of people watching a cock fight; let alone, sometimes, millions of other people watching twenty-two individuals, no more, running after a small melon-like sack full of air in meaningless movements.

In "The Village," on the other hand, he describes rural life as simple and peaceful. Out in the country, theft is nonexistent. "Abandon the city," Gadhafi writes. "Come to the village, where you can see the moon for the first time in your life-time, after you have changed from insignificant greedy worms and mice, void of social ties, to real human beings here, in the village, in the oasis, in the countryside."

One of the collection's high points is the short story "Suicide of the Astronaut," which recounts the life of a miserable astronaut who attempts to find work on Earth after arrogant superpowers no longer have the means to fund their expensive space programs. The astronaut discovers that his knowledge of astronomy is of little use when it comes to practical agriculture. After he has made some unsuccessful attempts at finding work, the story comes to its straightforward conclusion: "And so, having lost all hope of finding any bread-winning job on the Earth, the astronaut decided to commit suicide." Seldom has such a dramatic ending been so soberly written.

Of course, Gadhafi also put his many political musings on paper. His political masterpiece, *The Green Book*, is ambitiously subtitled: *The Solution of the Problem of Democracy. The Solution of the Economic Problem. The Social Basis of the Third Universal Theory.*

One would think that the solution to the democracy problem would be to found a dictatorship. Not so, according to Gadhafi. Instead, Western representative democracy is itself a form of dictatorship. "The party is a contemporary form of dictatorship," he writes. A political party represents only its members and fights for its own special interests. Democratically speaking, political parties should not be allowed to govern an entire people. The solution is what Gadhafi termed the

Third Universal Theory. Instead of electing parliamentary officials, people's committees should be established, which would be created and supervised by fundamental popular conferences. Representatives of the people's committees and popular conferences would all be assembled in what Gadhafi calls the "General People's Conference." This body would adopt resolutions that the people's committees and popular conferences would implement.

Obviously, this is significantly different from a legislative parliament. Furthermore, according to Gadhafi, every law passed haphazardly by any assembly, committee, or individual is undemocratic and unnatural. Only natural laws can be adopted. "The natural law of any society is grounded in either tradition (custom) or religion. Any other attempt to draft law outside these two sources is invalid and illogical," he writes. It can be objected that Gadhafi's political theory would tend to exclude himself as dictator, but luckily *The Green Book* leaves room for a strong man on top: "Theoretically, this is genuine democracy but, realistically, the strong always rules, i.e., the stronger party in the society is the one that rules." Touché!

The solution to the economic problem is simpler. As it turns out, paid labor enslaves workers. Accordingly, wages must be exchanged for a portion of the production itself. "The Social Basis for the Third Universal Theory" suggests that families are society's fundamental social unit and therefore the nation's building blocks. "The flourishing society is that in which the individual grows naturally within the family and the family within society," Gadhafi suggests. The recipe for a healthy family requires women to stay home and care for the children.

Gadhafi has also developed an interesting theory on sports. It is unacceptable to allow large masses of people to watch a small group of athletes compete. "Sports is like praying, eating, and the feelings of coolness and warmth. It is unlikely that crowds will enter a restaurant just to look at a person or a group of people eat," Gadhafi observes. Well put! As the deceased dictator also observes, when it comes to athletics, the most important component is participation: "When the masses march and play sport in the centre of playing fields and open spaces, stadiums will be vacant and become redundant. This will take place when the masses become aware of the fact that sport is a public activity which must be practiced rather than watched."

Education is also a part of the social basis in "The Social Basis for the Third Universal Theory," and here it must be admitted that Gadhafi's viewpoint is entirely liberal. The dictator believes that a society must offer all forms of education, and that everyone must have the opportunity to choose their own course of study. Gadhafi writes: "To force a human being to learn according to a set curriculum is a dictatorial act." He nonetheless succeeded in making his own political ideas a part of the school curriculum, showing what an exceptional pragmatist he was.

THE BOOK OF THE SOUL

The Green Book was obviously required material for a schoolchild in Libya, but unfortunately it was removed from the curriculum shortly after Gadhafi's death. Another dictatorial classic, which has likewise been removed from the school curriculum, is Saparmurat Miyazov's *Ruhnama: The Book of the Soul*. Under Turkmenbashi, *Ruhnama* was read by every student from kindergarten to the university. Questions on *Ruhnama* appeared on most exams, and Turkmen were required to recite long passages of the book from memory. All applicants for public positions were tested on *Ruhnama*, and one could occasionally expect to encounter questions from the book during a driver's test.

Because *Ruhnama* was such an important part of Turkmenistan's educational system, the authorities announced in 2004 that they were removing "some minor subjects, teachings, and scientific courses." Instead, the schools would emphasize the revival of local traditions and encourage a return to "natural spiritual values."

The first volume appeared in 2001 and is a combination of autobiography, history, politics, philosophy, and religion. In 2004, a second volume was published, containing a deeper moral and philosophical analysis and a number of writings on how a good Turkmen ought to behave. *Ruhnama* was also an important factor in Turkmenbashi's thoroughly developed personality cult. The romantic representation of Turkmenistan history meant that the book proved to be an important component in the building of Turkmenistan's national identity. Viewed in this light, Turkmenbashi can be said to be Turkmenistan's answer to the Brothers Grimm.

The book begins with an oath all Turkmen had to recite in order to prove their devotion to the president:

Turkmenistan, my beloved motherland, my beloved homeland!
You are always with me, in my thoughts and in my heart.
For the slightest evil against you, let my hand be lost!
For the slightest slander about you, let my tongue be lost!
At the moment of my betrayal to my motherland, to her sacred
    banner,
To Saparmurat Turkmenbashi the Great, let my breath stop!

In the first chapter, Turkmenbashi traces the origins of the Turkmen people five thousand years back, all the way back to the prophet Noah. Noah gave the Turkmen's land to his son, Jafet, and his descendants. God saw to it that the Turkmen received spiritual riches and courage as their distinctive characteristics. The next chapters narrate the history of Turkmen (which, surprisingly enough, have never been accurately represented by other historians), and the book culminates with the creation of the Turkmen national state, with Turkmenbashi as leader.

Because the book was first published in September, the month was renamed Ruhnama in honor of the president's masterwork. In Ashgabat, Turkmenbashi had a giant statue of the book erected. Similar to the rotating, thirty-foot-high gold statue of himself, the sculpture of Ruhnama is mechanical. Every evening, at eight o'clock, the cover opens and part of the text is played.

Having the book permeate every single aspect of Turkmen society was not enough for Turkmenbashi. In order to spread his message across the globe, foreign companies that wanted to do business in Turkmenistan were required to have the book translated into their native language. Therefore, *Ruhnama* has been translated into more than forty-one different languages, an endeavor financed by multinational corporations such as Siemens, Daimler-Chrysler, Caterpillar, and John Deere.

However, even that was not broad enough for Niyazov. In August 2005, a Russian rocket blasted a copy of the book into orbit—Turkmenbashi wanted to spread his wisdom to alien beings. Upon launch, the state newspaper *Neitralnyi Turkmenistan* wrote: "The book that conquered the hearts of millions on Earth is now conquering space." Also going into orbit with the book were the Turkmen flag and a picture of the presidential symbol, a five-headed eagle.

Turkmenbashi has proven to be an exceptional poet as well. In 2003, he won the Magtymguly International Prize, an award honoring Turkmenistan's national poet and given to the poet who best contributes to creating a Turkmen national state, one of Magtymguly's goals.

Turkmenbashi died in 2006, but his successor, Gurbanguly Berdymukhamedov, is also no stranger to the literary arts. Undoubtedly, his books on horses and plant medicine will, like *Ruhnama*, help create a personality cult around the president. The fact that both books deal with important phenomena in Turkmen culture is hardly coincidental. In 2011, it was announced that *Ruhnama* would be removed from school curricula and replaced with a book authored by the current president, entitled *Adamnama*, "Humanity's Book," and by September 2013, this had taken place.

SADDAM'S METAPHORS

One dictator who proved to be a prolific literary author is Saddam Hussein, who wrote five novels in the last years of his reign. Literary talent was in his genes. The dictator's uncle, Khairallah Talfah, former mayor of Baghdad, wrote the propaganda pamphlet "Three Whom God Should Not Have Created: Persians, Jews, and Flies." The book became a bestseller— probably because the authorities decreed that Iraq's twenty thousand schools had to buy fifty copies each. Otherwise, Talfah is famous for being so thoroughly corrupt that Hussein was forced to remove him from his position—no mean feat, considering the thoroughgoing corruption of Saddam's regime.

Hussein's first and most famous novel is *Zabibah and the King*, which was published in 2000. The book recounts the story of a king in medieval Iraq and a commoner named Zabibah. The king is fascinated by Zabibah's clever thoughts on politics and government, and eventually the two develop a romantic relationship. However, Zabibah is already unhappily married to an unsympathetic brute. Following a visit to the king, a masked man rapes her on her way home. The perpetrator later proves to be Zabibah's violent husband who wants to end the relationship, and the king takes revenge and declares war against the husband and his companions. In the end, both the king and his lover die.

After a time, it becomes obvious that the story is a metaphor, where Zabibah represents the Iraqi people, her evil husband is the United States, and the king is Saddam Hussein. Zabibah's rape occurs on January 17, the day the first Gulf War began. In contrast to the actual war, though, the symbolic American army in the book is conquered. The book became an instant bestseller in Iraq, with more than one million copies sold. Of course, the book's popularity could be because it was sold for about sixty cents when it was first published, and that in a dictatorship, it's a good rule of thumb to read the dictator's works. The novel was later dramatized in a television series with twenty episodes. A musical based on the book was also written.

Whether the Iraqi president actually wrote *Zabibah and the King* is not entirely clear. Many believe that Hussein hired a ghostwriter. It's been reported that the actual author was poisoned so the truth would never come to light. Of course, that is probably just a vicious rumor. Judging by the book's language, a professional author had nothing to do with it. The fact that Hussein continued to write after his imprisonment further proves that the dictator had true literary ambitions.

After his novel's jubilant reception, Hussein followed up with *The Fortified Castle*, a novel about a former soldier who falls in love with a Kurdish girl. His third novel, *Men and the City*, deals with the Ba'ath party's origins. Many of Hussein's relatives appear as characters in the book. His fourth novel, *Begone, Demons!*, appeared just before the American invasion in 2003. *Begone, Demons!* is about an Arab who fights against enemy tribes that symbolize Americans and Jews. Forty thousand copies were printed right before Baghdad fell.

Hussein wrote a novel with the working title *The Great Awakening* while he sat in jail after the war, but whether he finished the book before he was executed remains unknown. In any case, the book was never published. The Iraqi dictator also wrote poems in his cell. The magazine *Der Spiegel* has published the last poem, probably the last he ever wrote. It is entitled "Unbind Your Soul":

It is my soul mate and you are my soul's beloved.
No house could have sheltered my heart as you have.
The enemies forced strangers into our sea
And he who serves them will be made to weep.
Here we unveil our chests to the wolves
And will not tremble before the beast.
I sacrifice my soul for you and for our nation.
Blood is cheap in hard times.
We never kneel or bend when attacking,
But we even treat our enemy with honor.

AUTHORITARIAN FILM THEORY

The North Korean dictator Kim Il Sung also demonstrated exceptional literary talent. Among the high points, one finds the national romantic novel and opera, *Sea of Blood*, which concerns the resistance movement stationed at the foot of Mount Paektu during Japan's occupation of Korea. Telling the story of Japanese brutalities and North Korean heroic courage functions as a way to perfectly underpin King Il Sung's nationalistic ideology.

Sea of Blood was originally written as an opera. It is now one of the most popular operatic productions in North Korea and plays in Pyongyang several times a week. The story has also been made into a three-and-a-half-hour-long movie, in part directed by Kim Il Sung's son and successor, Kim Jong Il. Kim Jong Il was known to be a passionate movie buff. Supposedly, he had a private screening room with first-class audio and display equipment.

Like his father, Kim Jong Il produced an impressive amount of political literature. His most notable works are two books, *On the Art of Film* and *On the Art of Opera*, which provide a thorough introduction to the revolutionary performing arts. Kim Jong Il's opera theory is based on the groundbreaking staging of *Sea of Blood*. In his theory, Kim Jong Il emerges with some good, revolutionary advice: "A contemporary hero who appears in a work of art or literature must be a typical, independent and creative man who lives and works with an attitude befitting the master of the revolution and construction. The time is gone when the feudal emperors, aristocrats and millionaires were given prominence in operas."

Kim Jong Il's film theory encompasses both the artistic and political aspects of film production. When it comes to the artistic, Kim Jong Il insists, "a film without music is incomplete." Politically, the film should reflect the workers' revolution: "Political vision means seeing with the eye of the Party and judging all phenomena shrewdly from a revolutionary point of view."

One of Kim Jong Il's movie visions was to create a Korean version of *Godzilla*. Unfortunately, good directors were scarce in the Democratic People's Republic. In order to realize his dream, he ordered his security service to kidnap the South Korean director Shin Sang-ok. In January 1978, Shin's ex-wife, Choi Eun-hee, was kidnapped while she was in Hong Kong. She was placed on a boat and eight days later arrived in Nampo, North Korea. Kim Jong Il himself met her on the dock. The film enthusiast had a fantastically self-deprecating sense of humor. When he met Choi, he said, "I look like a sack of dwarf droppings, don't I?" Choi was then sent to a luxurious villa, and Kim Jong Il invited her to parties at his home.

When Shin arrived in Hong Kong to investigate the matter, he too was kidnapped. After several years of imprisonment, Shin agreed to make movies for Kim Jong Il. After the director was released, he was reunited with Choi, and at the suggestion of the film-loving dictator's son, they married again in North Korea. Shin directed seven movies in the country. The most famous is *Pulgasari*, the North Korean version of *Godzilla*, based on a Korean legend. In the movie, an evil king imprisons a blacksmith. Right before he starves to death, the blacksmith creates a rice doll, which transforms into a gigantic, metal-eating monster when it comes into contact with blood. Shin and Choi succeeded in fleeing from Kim Jong Il's captivity during a film festival in Vienna in 1986. Both were granted asylum in the United States, where Shin continued his directorial career.

AUTHORITARIAN SALES GIMMICKS

One of the advantages of being a dictator is that your books have a higher chance of becoming bestsellers. Putting your books in the school curriculum, like Turkmenbashi and Gadhafi did, is a great way to increase sales. Mao Zedong's *Quotations from Chairman Mao*, better known as *Mao's Little Red Book*, is one of world history's most-sold books, partially because all Chinese people were expected to have a copy on them at all times— something that proved useful when one encountered a difficult situation and needed advice from the wise leader, but also if one wanted to avoid arrest. However, *Mao's Little Red Book* also became a bestseller outside of China, mainly because radical Western youths would have dearly loved to recreate the beatific and forward-thinking Chinese dictatorship.

Exactly how many copies have been sold is uncertain, but the total is estimated to be around eight to nine hundred million. And that is only the number of copies sold—most have been given away. All told, more than six billion copies of the book have been printed, and it competes only with the Bible for having the greatest global circulation. Of course, most of Mao's works became bestsellers. According to historian Zhengyuan Fu, between 1966 and 1976 there were 1,820 state-owned printing houses in China that produced 6.5 billion copies of *Mao's Little Red Book*, 840 million copies of Mao Zedong's selected works in four volumes, 400 million copies of Mao's poems, and 2.2 billion placards with pictures of Mao. In light of all this, it is rather strange that Mao also published a book entitled *Oppose Book Worship*.

François "Papa Doc" Duvalier was a tad jealous of Mao's recognition as a political thinker. In order to prove his worth as ideologue and author, he published *Essential Works* in 1967. The book was an imitation of *Mao's Little Red Book*, but unfortunately, Papa Doc did not enjoy the same sales success as his literary hero. Still, Duvalier found a solution: he canceled the wages of all public employees and gave them a copy of his book instead.

8

KEEP STYLING

MOST STATE HEADS ARE CONCERNED about their appearance and choose their clothing with care. There are unwritten rules for acceptable attire at international meetings, gala dinners, national holidays, and other official events in which you might participate because of your position. Most politicians follow these rules. For that reason, their wardrobe is exceptionally dull, and it's almost impossible to distinguish one from the other. For men, tie color is generally the only thing that varies.

As a dictator, your wardrobe choices are far more forgiving than for your democratic colleagues. A quick look at dictatorial wardrobes over the last fifty years demonstrates a degree of imagination and variety that can compete with the most intrepid designers of Paris and Milan. A politician at the mercy of his constituents is obsessed with avoiding error and so will be reluctant to take chances with his clothing. A dictator, on the other hand, can dress as he pleases, without fearing critical backlash in the press the day after. In addition, it seems absolute power influences a person's aesthetic tastes. Power generates self-confidence and paves the way for experimentation.

As a general rule, the longer a dictator has occupied power, the more eccentric his style becomes. Just take a look at Muammar Gadhafi. The Libyan dictator was always vain, but at the beginning of his career, he largely confined himself to newly pressed uniforms. As the years progressed, he broadened his repertoire to include designer suits, Bedouin robes, and a number of other garments a less confident politician would never have donned. Even Robert Mugabe, who for years has stayed with anonymous, dull suits, has in the last few years begun to appear in colorfully printed shirts.

Despite significant individual variation, one can nonetheless pinpoint some general tendencies in the dictator dress code. The following five traditional fashion trends regularly adorn modern despots. Of course, there are exceptions, but most dictators in the last century fall into one of these categories.

The Classic

The classic dictator outfit is a stiff officer's uniform with impeccably ironed pants, marks of rank, and an elegant row of medals over the breast. While this style has proven popular on all continents, it is associated foremost with Latin American dictators such as Chile's Augusto Pinochet and Cuba's Fulgencio Batista.

Of course, it is no coincidence that a military uniform is popular among dictators. A large number of them have military backgrounds and have come to power through a military coup. A uniform broadcasts control and authority and sends an unmistakable signal to potential coup makers: *the finger on the button is mine.*

The Rebel

For some dictators, the classic uniform seems rather stiff. The rebellious dictator instead opts for a rocking, edgy variant. This is the despot version of the James Dean look. The rebel prefers a wrinkled uniform, with the jacket hanging open and the shirt's top buttons undone. Former guerrilla leaders are usually the ones who pick the rebel look.

The rebel style was partially developed because it is impractical to lug around an iron when you're conducting guerrilla warfare in the jungle. Still, the style undoubtedly attracts young revolutionary girls and is a conscientious clothing choice. The rebel sports a practical and comfortable style that broadcasts youth and the correct "who-gives-a-fuck" attitude.

Cuba's dictator Fidel Castro was a pioneering figure when it comes to this fashion trend. Another classic rebel is Thomas Sankara, who was the president of Burkina Faso from 1983 to 1987. Sankara's style choice led him to be dubbed Africa's Che Guevara. His wardrobe choice was obviously an expression of his vanity, and his shabby chic look was utterly premeditated. His uniforms were tailored, and he tended to carry a pistol with a mother-of-pearl handle.

The Peacock

Dictators enjoy bling. They enjoy gold statues, big cars, diamond-studded watches, and fancy interiors. Therefore, it comes as no surprise that some dictators cannot limit themselves to strict and sober uniforms. They would much prefer tassels, shiny medals, gold chains, colorful feathers, and lavish hats. Despots have a natural attraction to shiny objects, but those who embrace the peacock look throw every unwritten rule and all moderation overboard. Many dictators have begun with the classic uniform but developed an affinity for more extravagant attire as they aged, among them Paraguay's Alfredo Stroessner, Emperor Bokassa of the Central African Empire, and Sultan Hassanal Bolkiah of Brunei.

The Ethnic

Many dictators use their wardrobe to symbolize national pride, either by dressing in traditional attire or by using local traditions to create something new and progressive. King Mswati III of Swaziland is an example of a dictator who wavers between a purely traditional style and tailor-made modern suits. However, when he dons his ethnic dress, he goes all out. His outfits are distinguished by the extensive use of batik fabrics, exotic furs, colorful jewelry, and feathered headdresses. Dictators in the Middle East, such as King Abdullah of Saudi Arabia, are also drawn to traditional attire. There, their wardrobe serves a practical function as well: floor-length robes and fluttering headdresses keep one's body cool and shaded in the hot desert climate.

The Bores

In the last few decades, the military uniform has decreased in popularity. Dictators in former Soviet states, in particular, lack a military background and therefore cannot authentically dress in uniform. Unfortunately, the Western suit, complete with jacket and tie, has displaced most other outfits as the correct form of dress.

As a result, some dictators simply attempt to appear like normal politicians. They dress in dark gray and black prime-minister-style suits, white shirts, and monochrome ties, and at UN meetings are easily confused with straitlaced democrats like Jens Stoltenberg and Barack Obama. Uzbekistan's deceased despot, Islam Karimov, had an affinity for this style, as does Belarus's president since 1994, Aleksandr Lukasjenko. The same goes for the Chinese leaders, who haven't demonstrated an ounce of creative dictator fashion since Mao Zedong.

Of course, some dictators have such an eclectic style that they fall outside of any category. One of these was Muammar Gadhafi. The deceased Libyan dictator was always well dressed but experimented constantly with new garments and combinations. He dressed in everything from showy uniforms to traditional Bedouin attire, colorful silk outfits, and Miami Vice–inspired designer suits. According to Oksana Balinskaya, a Ukrainian nurse who worked for Gadhafi, the despot changed clothes multiple times a day. "He was so obsessive about his outfits that he reminded me of a rock star from the 1980s. Sometimes when his guests were already waiting for him, he would go back to his room and change his clothes again," Balinskaya told *Newsweek* in an interview in 2011.

Other dictators are so headstrong, they refuse to be pinned down. Kim Jong Il was a dictator who preferred to go his own way. In the course of his tenure, he almost always appeared in simple, short jackets, with elastic waistbands and matching pants, usually colored a neutral gray. This blend of uniform and tracksuit is comfortable and practical. Is it cold out? Well, throw the dictator into a large, gray bubble coat, not unlike the kind worn by employees of the Lillehammer Olympics in 1994. Kim Jong Il's wardrobe was also not without political symbolism. After he came to power, North Korea suffered several years of bad crops, and the population starved. By dressing plainly, the dictator showed sympathy for the people.

Kim Jong Il's Spartan style created waves in the international fashion world. The North Korean newspaper *Rodung Sinmun* reported in 2010 that Kim Jong Il had become an international trendsetter: "The reason is that the august image of the Great General, who is always wearing the modest suit while working, leaves a deep impression on people's mind in the world." This claim was supported by international fashionistas: "Kim Jong Il mode [sic], which is now spreading expeditiously worldwide, is something unprecedented in the world's history," an anonymous French fashion expert told the party paper.

Dictators are not only vain on their own account. Oftentimes they dictate how their subordinates should dress. The fact that a dictator desires a well-dressed populace is a sympathetic trait, but such mandates may have a practical side as well. Clothing may be utilized as part of the official state ideology or the obligatory personality cult. Thomas Sankara is just one of many dictators who have tried to nationalize the country's dress code. He ordered all public employees in Burkina Faso to wear traditional garments woven from local cotton and sewn by local tailors.

The "Mao suit" is more famous. In China, the outfit is typically called the Zhongshan suit and was basically inspired by Japanese uniforms. Adopted by the People's Liberation Army and by party members, it acquired the name "Mao suit" when Mao Zedong began wearing it.

The suit is a perfect expression of Mao's ideology. It is practical, designed along simple lines, and composed of a solid and sensible cotton fabric. The suit consists of pants and a jacket with four external pockets in front and comes in blue and green. Combined with the elegant Mao cap, a brim cap adorned with a small red star on front, the suit fits most occasions, whether for a party or for work. The outfit is practical, it symbolizes equality and simple, pedestrian values, and it can be worn by both men and women. During the Cultural Revolution, almost all Chinese males wore this uniform. In the 1990s, the Mao suit, the outfit for all occasions, was replaced by the dull, and much less attractive, international businessman's attire.

The Mao suit was copied by almost all other communist dictators. Pol Pot, the leader of Cambodia's Khmer Rouge, adopted a similar outfit. North Korea's first dictator, Kim Il Sung, also wore a Mao-inspired uniform. Mobutu Sese Seko looked to the Mao suit when it came time to design a proper national costume for the Congolese people. During the so-called Zairization of Congolese society in the 1970s, the dictator needed a substitute for imperialistic Western suits. He changed the country's name from Congo to Zaire and forbade the wearing of suits with shirts and ties. Instead, the inhabitants could use abacost jackets—a light and thin jacket with long or short sleeves—which was well-suited to Congo's tropical climate.

This garment was introduced after Mobutu visited China and met Mao in 1973. The Mao suit's inspiration is obvious. The word "abacost" comes from the French à bas le costume, which means "down with the suit." Some might point out the contradiction inherent in promoting a Chinese-inspired jacket with a French name as national Congolese attire, but they simply misinterpret Mobutu's fashion vision. A pure traditional garb would have been difficult in a country like the Congo, which has such a plethora of diverse ethnic groups. Mobutu's own fashion trademark was a leopard-skin cap which, worn in tandem with his self-designed abacost jacket and Buddy Holly glasses, proved to be a fusion of Congolese history and modern youth culture.

ARCHITECTONIC MASTERPIECES

It is not only wardrobe choice that distinguishes dictators from the world's other heads of state. When it comes to architecture, there are also clear commonalities among different authoritarian regimes. One thing that characterizes authoritarian architecture is the idea that size matters. Of course, large structures are built in democratic lands too, but the basis for big thinking is different in dictatorships than in democracies.

New York's skyscrapers are a source of pride to the city's inhabitants, but in principle, they are high because space is scarce in Manhattan. When a dictator builds skyscrapers, it is because he can build them as much as because the country needs them. Despots have the advantage that, in a dictatorship, the construction of public buildings is not subject to the same social debate as in democracies.

"Big" is often equated with threatening, and many people believe that totalitarian architecture is gigantic simply to demonstrate the regime's power and the subjects' powerlessness. However, these theories undervalue the fact that gigantic architecture exhibits progress, pride, and community. More than emphasizing how puny the individual inhabitants are, grandiose architecture underscores the magnificence of the individual who is fortunate enough to be a part of such a magnificent nation.

What dictators build should ideally be larger and better than whatever they take as their template. In honor of Kim Il Sung's seventieth birthday in 1982, a triumphal arch was built in Pyongyang. The arch is a replica of Paris's Arc de Triomphe and is meant to symbolize the dictator's resistance to the Japanese occupation. Of course, the arch is slightly higher than the original French arch. The two-hundred-foot-tall monument is built of 25,500 granite blocks, one for each day in the Great Leader's life up to that point. Naturally, a mere monument was not enough to adequately celebrate such an important occasion as the president's seventieth birthday. A tower was also erected in honor of the Juche ideology, the 558-foot-tall Juche Tower. The monument is three feet taller than the Washington Monument and is built of granite blocks—again, one for every day of Kim Il Sung's life. At the top is a nearly seventy-foot-tall, forty-five-ton glowing metal torch.

One of the most fascinating dictator structures is the basilica in Yamoussoukro. President Félix Houphouët-Boigny of the Ivory Coast began building this monster church in the city of his birth in 1985. In 1989, it seized the record as the world's largest church from the previous title holder, St. Peter's in the Vatican. The basilica is obviously inspired by St. Peter's, but in contrast to it, the president's basilica is built largely of concrete. The church is 518 feet tall, comprises an area of 323,000 square feet, and has room for 18,000 people. Seventy-five thousand square feet of colored glass were imported from France to create the stained glass windows. One such window shows Houphouët-Boigny as one of the three kings who are extending gifts to Jesus. An accompanying villa to the church is reserved for papal visits. The villa has been used only once, in 1990, when Pope John Paul II blessed the church.

CITY PLANNING PAR EXCELLENCE

A couple of palaces and some paltry skyscrapers might not be enough. If you really want to pull out all the stops as dictator, your own city is a must-have. It is not unusual, of course, for dictators to name cities after themselves. Joseph Stalin had Stalingrad, and Omar Bongo dubbed his birth town Bongoville. However, some dictators are not content to merely attach their name to an already existing city—they prefer to build one from scratch.

Haiti's dictator François "Papa Doc" Duvalier was one of them. He needed a display window to show the world how progressive and modern Haiti had become under his rule. In 1961, the sleepy rural town of Cabaret was chosen as the place to have the honor of being shaped in Papa Doc's image. In the speech given to announce the official decision, Papa Doc promised the inhabitants that the town would become a jewel and that he himself would have a residence there. He set in motion a number of gigantic building projects and changed the town's name from Cabaret to Duvalierville. In order to finance the projects, large companies were asked to contribute economic support. Those who refused found the Tonton Macoutes, Duvalier's security force, breathing down their necks. Even schoolchildren were encouraged to give "voluntary" contributions. Unfortunately, the city was never finished. In fact, most of the building projects were never even started, and in 1986, when Duvalier's son, Baby Doc, fled Haiti, the town changed its name back to Cabaret.

Faith can move mountains, as Jesus declared in the Book of Mark. While that remark may seem overly confident in the power of faith, it does at least seem that superstition can move capitals. In Burma, it is generally accepted that the capital was changed from Yangon to the newly established city of Naypyidaw after the military junta's chief astrologer warned of an external attack. The official explanation for the capital's relocation was that Yangon was getting too cramped, there was not enough room to build new governmental offices, and the junta wished to have a more centrally located capital. Yangon, for its part, is on the coast. On November 6, 2006, at 6:37 a.m., a time Burmese astronomy considers auspicious, the government began shifting its departments to Naypyidaw, and the city officially became Burma's capital.

Naypyidaw, which loosely translates to "royal" or "the king's seat," is one of the world's most organized cities. People are settled according to profession and civil status. The apartment blocks have color-coded roofs to signal the residents' type of employment. Blocks housing residents who work in the Ministry of Health have a blue roof, whereas blocks housing employees of the Ministry of Agriculture and Irrigation have green roofs.

Government workers have their own district. High-ranking officers live in a military zone six miles removed from other government employee housing. Roads leading to the military zone have eight lanes and can double as airstrips for small planes. Within the ministry zone, the various ministries keep to their respective identical buildings. The members of parliament occupy an enormous complex consisting of thirty-one buildings. The presidential palace, which has one hundred rooms, is also located in the ministry zone. The city boasts a hotel zone and an embassy zone. Naypyidaw's building plan is perfect for a dictatorship. The city has no public places where large groups can gather to protest—it does not even have a defined center. The wide streets have next to no traffic. Visitors have described the city as being almost as empty as a ghost town.

Another dictator who has shifted his capital to a more central location is Kazakhstan's president, Nursultan Nazarbayev. In 1997, he moved the capital from Almaty to the city of Akmola, in the middle of the Kazakh Steppe. The following year, he changed the city's name to Astana, which literally means "capital." The official reasons for the capital's relocation were that Almaty was located in an earthquake zone, it had poor geographic growth opportunities, and it was located too near the border with Kyrgyzstan. It has also been claimed that moving the capital farther north enables the government to better control Kazakhstan's Russian populace, which mostly inhabits the northern regions.

Foreigners, however, were not as enthused about Astana as President Nazarbayev. Businesspeople and tourists continued to favor the old capital of Almaty. In order to underscore how important it was to recognize Astana as the capital, for a time Kazakhstan prohibited foreign airlines from flying directly into Almaty. They were allowed to fly to the old capital only if the plane first stopped in Astana.

Financed by Kazakhstan's oil revenues, Astana has grown into a modern city with tall glass and steel buildings. A number of grandiose architectural projects have been set in motion. Of course, an enormous presidential palace, called Ak Orda ("The White Horde"), was built and topped with a massive dome and 262-foot-tall spire. At the cupola's pinnacle stands a sculpture representing the sun with thirty-two rays and a steppe eagle in flight beneath it.

Even more spectacular is the Palace of Peace and Reconciliation. The 253-foot-tall pyramid was constructed to house the Congress of Leaders of World and Traditional Religions, one of Nazarbayev's brainchildren. The congress has the noble purpose of encouraging constructive dialogue between civilizations, faiths, countries, and peoples. Every three years, two hundred leaders from the world's most important faiths and religions meet in a round conference room, built as a large copy of the United Nations Security Council's meeting room. Because the pyramid is so massive, there is also space for an opera theater with 1,500 seats in the structure's lowest part. Who says that dictators always have nefarious intentions?

Nazarbayev is also responsible for the world's largest concert hall, which has 3,500 seats and was designed by the famous Italian architect Manfredi Nicoletti. Its shape is inspired by flower petals, and it is covered in glass painted the colors of the Kazakh flag.

Nonetheless, Astana's most impressive structure is probably Khan Shatyr. It is the world's largest tent and is practically its own city district. It is a transparent canvas supported by a 490-foot-tall pole, covering an area larger than ten soccer fields. The tent houses a park, cobbled shopping streets, a river, a miniature golf course, and an artificial beach. The tent is constructed to maintain an even and comfortable temperature year-round, which is extremely practical in a city that oscillates between scorching summers and freezing winters.

One of Astana's most important landmarks is Bayterek, meaning "the tall poplar." At 344 feet, the tower is actually a sculpture based on a local folk legend. According to the tale, a bird laid her egg in the branches of the "Tree of Life." Bayterek's top appropriately spreads itself into several branches that encompass a gold-colored egg, 130 feet in diameter. The egg contains an observer platform exactly ninety-seven meters (318 feet) above the ground, a reference to the fact that Astana became the capital in 1997. On the observer platform is a gold-plated print of Nazarbayev's right hand. A small plaque off to the side proclaims that whoever places his hand over the president's handprint will have a wish granted. When you do this, Kazakhstan's national anthem plays.

In 2008, the Kazakh parliament suggested naming the city after the president and changing Astana to Nursultan. Surprisingly, Nazarbayev rejected the suggestion, but many believe he wants the city to change its name when he either dies or retires.

Astana has some of the world's most magnificent buildings. But if none of them piques your interest, there is, of course, a museum dedicated to President Nazarbayev for your enjoyment.

THE GHOST TOWN

Duvalierville, Naypyidaw, and Astana are all cities designed to be inhabited by people (even if the dictators behind them built them as self-memorials as well). North Korea, in contrast, had completely different motives for building the small town of Kijŏngdong not too far from the demilitarized zone between North and South Korea. In North Korea, Kijŏngdong is also known as Peace Village, while South Koreans prefer to call it Propaganda Town. Officially, the town is designed for two hundred families who manage a collective farm. It has a kindergarten, secondary schools, and a hospital. When Kijŏngdong was built in the 1950s, its apartment blocks with blue-painted roofs and working electricity were of a much higher standard than most of North Korea's other rural towns.

The amazing thing is that none of this is real. The town is the only settlement in North Korea that is visible from the South Korean side of the demilitarized zone. However, with strong binoculars one can see that the houses are only shells, without glass in the windows or interior rooms. The lights in the buildings are turned off and on at scheduled times to maintain the illusion that someone lives there. The only human activity is the occasional street sweeper, who serves to maintain the appearance of habitation. The town was most likely built for propaganda reasons, to show South Koreans how great things are on the North Korean side.

It is lucky that no one lives there, though, because the sound levels would be unbearable. Powerful loudspeakers pointed at the South Korean border broadcast propaganda messages up to twenty hours a day. At the beginning, they were messages attempting to encourage South Korean soldiers to defect. Since surprisingly few were tempted across the border, North Koreans have instead started playing anti-imperialistic speeches full-blast, interspersed with nationalistic opera and military music.

During the 1980s, South Korea, which at the time was also a dictatorship, raised a 323-foot flagstaff with a 287-pound South Korean flag in the city of Daeseong-dong on the other side of the demilitarized zone. North Korea could do no less, so they hoisted their own 525-foot flagstaff with a 595-pound flag in Kijŏngdong. This has often been referred to as the Flagstaff or Flagpole War. The flagstaff in Kijŏngdong is currently the world's fourth largest. It might appear that dictators have a fetish for flagstaffs—perhaps it is compensation for small penises, who knows? In any case, the world's tallest flagstaff is found in another dictatorship. It is located in Jeddah, Saudi Arabia, and is 558 feet tall. Next comes one in Tajikistan's capital city, Dushambe, which is 541 feet tall and supports a 100-by-200-foot Tajik flag. The world's next-tallest flagstaff

(531 feet) is in Azerbaijan, whereas the fifth tallest (436 feet) is in Turkmenistan.

THE LANDSCAPE ARCHITECT

It is one thing to build new cities but quite another to alter nature. Emir Mohammed bin Rashid Al Maktoum of Dubai obviously believes the Persian Gulf emirate over which he rules is too small. Therefore, he has initiated various large projects designed to increase the emirate's dimensions and coastline. In 2001, construction was started on the first of three artificial peninsulas. The peninsulas look like palm trees, each of them surrounded by a crescent-shaped island. The two smallest, Palm Jumeirah and Palm Jebel Ali, will consist of 81,000 acre feet (100 million cubic meters) of sand and stone, whereas the largest, Palm Deira, will consist of 811,000 acre feet (one billion cubic meters) of building material. As a finished product, Palm Deira was supposed to house up to one million inhabitants, but the plans were scaled back during construction due to unanticipated technical difficulties. The peninsulas are also supposed to hold hotels, luxury villas, water parks, restaurants, and shopping centers. However, the project's future is in doubt, as the 2008 financial crisis brought much of the construction to a halt.

The Palm Islands' developer is the state-controlled entrepreneurial firm, the Nakheel Company. In addition to the Palms, they will also construct two artificial island groups, called the World and the Universe. In the World, the islands will be shaped like a world atlas, whereas the Universe will be a copy of the solar system and the Milky Way Galaxy. (For the time being, the Universe has been put on hold.) The islands in the World will be shaped like individual countries or cities. It was the emir himself who dreamed up and initiated the project. Even though many of the islands have been sold, the development has not gone as smoothly as the emir had foreseen. Property prices have fallen substantially since their peak right before the 2008 financial crisis, and it has been claimed that the islands are in the process of sinking into the sea, with the water between them clogging with sediment—a claim Nakheel denies.

Dubai's artificial islands just go to show that even a dictator can make mistakes. The enormous sums of money being pumped into Emir Mohammed's prestige project have contributed to the sinking of the dictator's fortune, from $16 billion in 2007 to only $4 billion in 2011. Playing God is fun, but it does come with a price.

9

SHARE THE BENEFITS (WITH YOUR FRIENDS)

THE DICTATOR LIFESTYLE IS NOT necessarily limited to dictators. Sometimes, it's enough to be related to one. Siblings, spouses, and children of dictators all generally occupy privileged positions in authoritarian countries. Dictator family members exist above the law, they are first in line when there are business opportunities or natural resources to dole out, and they wield political influence, which is reserved for only a tiny portion of the populace in most dictatorships.

Indeed, in many ways it is better to be related to a dictator than to be the actual dictator. You receive a wealth of benefits without having to shoulder the heavy responsibility of state leadership. On the other hand, you miss out on the remarkable rush that comes from unlimited authority over others, the possibility to shape a country in your own image, and the joy of being worshipped like a god. Both sides have their ups and downs.

ACADEMIC SHORTCUTS

Being a member of the dictator's family is a sure pathway to a great job, and a lack of qualifications is certainly no hindrance. The position doesn't necessarily even require you to work or show up at the office. Receiving a paycheck is more than sufficient.

Elena Ceaușescu, wife of Romania's dictator Nicolae Ceaușescu, had no particular education. She dropped out of school when she was fourteen years old, after having failed most subjects. The only subjects she passed were handwork, choir, and gym. When she was done with school, Elena traveled to her brother's home in Bucharest. In the capital, she found a job working as an assistant in a questionable lab that produced diet pills and headache tablets. The job was short-lived but awakened her interest in chemistry. Later, she found a position at a textile factory. In 1937, she became a member of the Communist Party, and she met her Nicolae a couple of years later. They were married in 1947.

Elena worked for a time as a secretary in Romania's Ministry of Foreign Affairs before being fired for incompetence. She began an evening course in chemistry but was tossed out for cheating on an exam. Elena's career prospects certainly did not appear promising. Luckily, she had a husband who could help.

Nicolae's eventual ascent up Romania's power hierarchy paved the way for Elena's brilliant career as a chemist. In 1960, she received a doctorate in chemistry, an impressive feat for someone who hardly had any theoretical training. In 1965, she became the head of ICECHIM, Romania's National Institute for Research and Development in Chemistry and Petrochemistry. She was dubbed a "world-famous chemist and researcher" in official newspapers. A number of scientific articles written by other scientists were published under her name. Employees at the National Institute have said that no one could publish anything without Elena's name at the top, even though often she couldn't pronounce all the words in the article. For her part, Elena complained that, given her stellar publication record, she was never nominated for the Nobel Prize in Chemistry.

When she traveled abroad with her husband, she always tried to find a university in the host country that would give her an honorary degree. Romania's premier intelligence agency, Departamentul de Informatii Externe (DIE), had orders to negotiate with prestigious research institutions to ensure the first lady received academic honors.

In 1975, Elena became Doctor Honoris Causa at the University of Tehran and at Jordan's university in Amman. When the Ceaușescus visited Great Britain in 1978, Oxford and Cambridge were asked if they, too, would bestow honorary titles on the dictator's wife. Both respectfully declined. Nonetheless, Central London Polytechnic and Royal Institute of Chemistry were happy to play along and honor Elena's natural academic talent.

During a visit to Washington, DC, that same year, no university in the region was willing to acknowledge Elena's scientific merits. Instead, she had to content herself with a membership in the Illinois Academy of Science. She was manifestly galled that President Jimmy Carter couldn't muster a degree for her from some Washington institution: "You can't sell me the idea that Mr. Peanut [Carter] can give me an Illiwhatsis diploma but not any from Washington. I will not go to Illiwhatever-it-is. *I will not!*" She later complained that she had never heard of Illinois and protested that she was expected to accept such an insignificant token from a "dirty Jew," referring to Emanuel Merdinger, the then head of the Illinois Academy of Science.

Before a trip to the Philippines, DIE beseeched President Ferdinand Marcos to convince the University of Manila to give Elena an honorary doctorate in exchange for a significant monetary donation. The dictator's wife wouldn't admit that this honor was due entirely to the intelligence agency. She said as much to the DIE chief who had secured her the title: "I don't think you know, darling, but their university insisted on giving me an honorary doctorate. I kept refusing, but do you know what they did? They may be little yellow people, but they made Imelda [Marcos] take me there. What could I do then, darling?"

However, Elena wasn't satisfied with having only an academic career. She also wanted a powerful political position. On a 1971 trip to China, when she saw that Mao Zedong's wife, Jiang Qing, had acquired an important and powerful position, she was inspired to take more ambitious political posts. As usual, sleeping with the boss helps, and the dictator's wife was eventually given a number of key offices. In 1972, she became a member of the Communist Party's Central Committee. In 1977, she became a member of the Permanent Bureau of the Political Executive Committee, the Communist Party's highest body, and in March 1980, she became first deputy prime minister.

GLAM SISTERS

Islam Karimov occupied power in Uzbekistan from when the former Soviet Republic became independent in 1991 until his death in 2016. He was most famous for boiling his enemies alive and for working closely with Washington, DC, in the so-called War on Terror. The Uzbek dictator had two beautiful, glamorous daughters who combined the sweet jet-setting lifestyle with brilliant diplomatic careers.

Karimov's oldest daughter, Gulnara Karimova, is, or perhaps was—in 2016 it was rumored that she had died by poisoning while under house arrest, not long after the death of her father—something of a Renaissance person. During her heyday, she was a businesswoman, diplomat, academic, singer, and jewelry and clothing designer. American diplomats described her as "glamorous and highly controversial," not to mention "the most hated person in the country," according to documents published by WikiLeaks.

Gulnara studied economics at Tashkent University and earned a master's degree from Harvard University and a doctorate in political science at the Tashkent University of World Economy and Diplomacy, where she had a professorship. How much time Gulnara devoted to her academic duties is uncertain, as she had a number of other projects that she seemed to prioritize—such as her career as a pop star. She launched her first music video in 2006, under the stage name GooGoosha, which was her father's nickname for her. The song is called "Unutma Meni," or "Don't Forget Me." She also released the song "Besame Mucho" with Julio Iglesias. In 2012, she released her first album with the same singer, based on her own personal experiences. That same year she was featured in the song and music video "The Sky Is Still" with French actor Gérard Depardieu.

Gulnara's creative side emerged in various ways. At New York's Fashion Week in 2010, she showed her line of self-designed clothes, inspired by Uzbek fabrics and patterns, under the trademark Guli. In 2011, she planned to return to Fashion Week, but was dumped by the arrangers following a campaign led by Human Rights Watch. The human rights organization contended that Gulnara shouldn't be allowed to advertise Uzbek clothing while children in Uzbekistan were taken out of school two months a year to pick cotton. She also designed a jewelry line, and in 2009 launched the collection Guli for Chopard in association with the renowned Swiss company Chopard.

One may wonder how Gulnara found time for the music and clothing design, given her diplomatic career. She served in Uzbekistan's United Nations delegation in New York and worked at the Uzbek embassy in Moscow. In 2008, she became the deputy foreign minister and later that same year was appointed to be Uzbekistan's representative in Geneva's UN office. In 2010, she became ambassador to Spain, though she still kept her position in Geneva. Beginning in 2005, this multitalented woman was the director of the Uzbek think tank, Center for Political Studies.

Gulnara has also developed an interest in sports. She financed the soccer club Bunyodkor, which, in an attempt to raise Uzbekistan's status as a soccer country, has bought a number of high profile Brazilian players, among others the superstar Rivaldo. In the Asian Champions League, Bunyodkor has a good showing, but the club is not popular on the home field. In a match with the significantly poorer club Pakhtakor ("Cotton Pickers"), which consists entirely of Uzbek players, Bunyodkor was beaten 1-0, partially because most of the Brazilian players were given red cards in the first ten minutes. According to a report from the American embassy in Tashkent, the head referee telephoned Bunyodkor's trainer after the match and explained that he was sorry, but that he must provide for his family. The referee had received an order from the president of the Uzbekistan Football Federation to let Pakhtakor win 1-0. It might seem strange that the football federation would work against a club in which the president's daughter had an investment, but the match had no significance for Bunyodkor's position in the Asian league rankings. On the home field, most Uzbeks still cheer for Uzbek players, so the outcome may have been intended to appease local fans. However, there may also have been another motivation here: the ambassador's report observes that the result probably affected what bookies would pay out due to the long odds associated with a Pakhtakor win.

Gulnara demonstrated the advantage of being a dictator's family member when one is going through a bitter divorce. She married the Afghani-American businessman Mansur Maqsudi in 1991. Maqsudi opened a Coca-Cola company in Uzbekistan's capital, Tashkent. The couple had two children before the relationship soured. When the marriage began to crumble in 2001, their divorce became an international scandal. Many of Maqsudi's family members in Uzbekistan were arrested, and others were chased across the Afghanistan border. Maqsudi's Uzbek enterprises suddenly found themselves in trouble.

A month after the separation, the authorities began creating problems for the Coca-Cola Company in Tashkent. Tax inspectors, customs inspectors, even anti-drug agents played their part. The whole affair ended with the Coca-Cola plant being forced to close its doors within four months, and Maqsudi losing both that factory and other Uzbekistan investments. Arrest warrants were issued for Maqsudi, his brother, and his father, with accusations of tax evasion, corruption, and oil deals made with Saddam Hussein. The authorities in Uzbekistan deny that this had anything to do with the divorce.

Although Gulnara was happy to display her musical and artistic talents in the media, she was less willing to disclose her other business enterprises. Most Uzbekistan watchers assume she had an enormous fortune. The Swiss magazine *Bilanz* suggested that she was one of the ten richest people in Switzerland, with an estimated fortune of around $600 million. She supposedly controlled the Uzbek industry giant Zeromax, which was a key player in the country's petroleum sector, mining operations, agriculture, textile industry, and banking sector. Zeromax is registered in Switzerland, where the dictator's daughter lived, but so far, no one has succeeded in finding concrete evidence of her ownership in the company. A series of reports by the Swedish television channel SVT provided some insight into Gulnara's business methods, and it seems she employed certain dictatorial techniques. SVT acquired a number of documents that indicated the dictator's daughter received $250 million in bribes from the Swedish telecommunications company Telia-Sonera to allow them to enter the Uzbek market.

The revelation set in motion a series of events that demonstrate that even a dictator's daughter can fall from power. Up until that point, everything seemed to be going beautifully for the talented young woman. In 2013, she organized Style.UZ Art Week, an annual festival for fashion, art, film, theater, and music in Uzbekistan's capital, Tashkent, which doubled as Gulnara's annual opportunity to show herself among the world's jet set. That year, the high points included a fashion show with the Canadian designer duo DSquared2 and a Hello Kitty nail design workshop. The festival was so prominent that it even attracted participants from outer space: during the opening ceremony, three Russian astronauts sent a greeting from the International Space Station.

Around the same time, a Karimov family feud erupted into an open squabble in Western media and on the Internet. Islam Karimov's youngest daughter, Lola Karmova-Tillyaeva, declared in an interview with the BBC that she hadn't spoken to her big sister Gulnara in twelve years and that she doubted Gulnara had any chance of assuming power in Uzbekistan. Gulnara responded by accusing her sister of black magic: "One part of the family (the father) provides, the other destroys with the help of sorcerers," she wrote on Instagram. She followed this by accusing her sister of embezzlement and of destroying religious inscriptions during the renovation of an orphanage. She implied that her mother, Tatiana Karimova, also practiced witchcraft: "Who knows anything about the strange practice of making star- and triangle-shaped candle installations and constantly repeating something?" Gulnara asked on Twitter. She then expressed concern for her mother.

That same month, Akbarali Abdullayev, nephew of Karimov's wife and Gulnara's close ally, was arrested for embezzlement, corruption, and tax evasion. The arrest prompted Gulnara to storm into the office of the head of National Security, Rustam Inoyatov, and berate him as she kicked doors and office furniture: "Are you a man or not? Put a skirt on your fat ass. Understood?" she apparently shouted.

The dictator, Islam Karimov, had apparently been unaware of the extent of his daughter's corruption, as a meeting with the security head demonstrates. Inoyatov showed him pictures of his daughter posing half naked and documents proving the extent of Gulnara's questionable business dealings. Karimov was so outraged that he threw an ashtray and a telephone at the security chief. He summoned all of his closest aides and accused them of withholding information about his daughter. He then ordered that everyone who dealt with corruption in the National Security Office and the Ministry of Internal Affairs be arrested if they had had the slightest knowledge of any of his daughter's shady financial dealings.

After that, the president apparently called Gulnara to the carpet and slapped her. He continued to beat her, accusing her of shaming the family before the whole world. It got so violent that Karimov's bodyguards attempted to calm him. Later, the dictator was observed weeping in the gardens of the presidential palace.

Many of Gulnara's bank accounts were closed and the stores she owned in Tashkent were shuttered. According to Gulnara's son, Islam Karimov, Jr., the family held a meeting on January 2, 2014, at which the president vented his anger at his daughter's use of Twitter and continued Internet presence. He accused Gulnara of ruining Uzbekistan's reputation. From that point on, the unfortunate daughter lived under house arrest and had limited contact with the outside world. When the rumor emerged in November 2016 that she had died of poisoning within two months of her father's death following a stroke, her son challenged authorities to "Show the world my mum is alive," while accusing the Uzbek security services of keeping her isolated. The moral of the story is clear: if you earn millions through corruption, hide it adequately and, above all, make sure you have the dictator's blessing.

The Uzbek president could thank his youngest daughter, Lola Karimova-Tillyaeva, for the fact that he was the world's only head of state with a court ruling recognizing him as a dictator. As her older sister was, Lola is a diplomat, and like Gulnara she received her education from the University for World Economy and Diplomacy in Tashkent. In addition, she holds a doctorate in psychology from Tashkent State University. She is Uzbekistan's permanent representative at UNESCO's main office in Paris but spends much of her time hanging out with celebrities at charity events.

An article in the French Internet newspaper Rue89 described Lola as a dictator's daughter who used charitable events to whitewash Uzbekistan's image. Rue89 pointed out that Lola's big sister, Gulnara, had participated in the charitable event Cinema Against AIDS during the Cannes Film Festival, while only a few months earlier an activist in Uzbekistan had been sentenced to seven years in prison for distributing a brochure about how to protect oneself against HIV. Lola deemed the article defamatory and sued the paper for 30,000 euros in damages. The court ruled that, while the contents of the brochure stood "contrary to the mentality and moral basis of the Uzbek people's society, religion, culture and traditions," the article was entirely in keeping with reality. Lola's suit against Rue89 was dismissed.

THE PLAYBOY PRINCE

A dictator has enemies everywhere. As such, paranoia is a natural occupational hazard among despots, rather than proof of a predisposition to mental disorders in the dictator class. Even one's family is not to be trusted. Sometimes, family members prove the greatest threat of all.

Francisco Macías Nguema was the son of a witch doctor in Spanish Guinea, a microcolony located on Africa's west coast, in what one might term Africa's armpit. The country, which is now called Equatorial Guinea, consists of an island and a small strip of mainland. At one point, the country was an important exporter of cocoa, but now, billions of dollars stream in from the oil fields found in the nearby sea. Francisco was certainly no egghead, but he nonetheless succeeded in finding a job as mayor under the Spanish administration in the city of Mongomo, despite failing the civil service exam three times. He quickly rose through the ranks and eventually became deputy prime minister in the West African colony.

In September 1968, Nguema was elected president in the country's first and only free election. On October 12, 1968, the country became independent and changed its name to Equatorial Guinea, and Nguema quickly saw the chance to assume total control of the young state. His opponent in the presidential election was accused of a coup attempt and executed. In 1971, Nguema changed the constitution so that he received "all direct powers of Government and Institutions," giving him authority over all legislative and judicial powers, in addition to being head of the government and state.

To insult the president was forbidden. Breaking this law could result in up to thirty years' imprisonment. To threaten the president was punishable by death. In 1972, Nguema united all the country's political parties under the United National Party (later renamed the United National Workers' Party). He declared himself president for life of both party and country. In 1973, he introduced a new constitution that awarded the president absolute power and gave legal grounding to the one-party system. In a referendum on July 29, 1973, 99 percent of the populace voted to adopt the new constitution.

To protect himself against enemies, Nguema filled all the country's key positions with his relatives. Strange as it may seem, the rest of the populace didn't quite understand how good they had it under Nguema's rule. A third of Equatorial Guinea's inhabitants fled the country during the course of Nguema's rule, including his wife, who disappeared from the country in 1976. Out of three hundred thousand inhabitants, up to one hundred thousand were murdered. In order to halt the exodus, Nguema prohibited fishing and destroyed the coastal people's boats. He also forbade Western medicine and the use of the word "intellectual." His poor results in school had obviously given him a deep skepticism toward educated people. Nonetheless, the dictator called himself the Grandmaster of Science, Education, and Culture.

In 1975, 150 people were arrested and accused of plotting a coup. The alleged coup makers were executed in a stadium in the capital Mabako, while a band played "Those Were the Days." After taking the life of the chief of the Central Bank, Nguema moved all the bank's valuables to his house in his hometown, a rural village.

He ordered all churches to conclude all worship services with the chant "Forward with Macías, always with Macías, never without Macías," and he later prohibited Catholicism in general. Priests were either killed or imprisoned. In 1978, Nguema changed the country's motto to "There is no other God than Macías Nguema."

Even though his onetime political opposition had been eradicated and his own family occupied all important government positions, Nguema still didn't feel safe. During the summer of 1979, he executed many of his own family members. That was a mistake. On August 3, his own nephew, Deputy Prime Minister Teodoro Obiang Nguema Mbasogo, replaced him. Macías Nguema was imprisoned after he attempted to hide out in the jungle with a handful of loyal soldiers. On September 29, the ex-dictator was sentenced to death 101 times and executed (only once) at the jail at six o'clock that same afternoon.

Teodoro Mbasogo took over as president of the country, and it wasn't long before he showed himself to be almost as authoritarian as his uncle. Mbasogo, however, is a more cultivated man than his predecessor. He plays exceptional tennis, and those who meet him describe him as polite and sympathetic. With the discovery of oil in the sea off Equatorial Guinea's coast, the way to international recognition and respect was opened.

Oil has given Mbasogo clear advantages. First, when it comes to human rights abuses, the oil-thirsty United States tends to look the other way while at the same time cultivating international legitimacy for Mbasogo's regime. Second, oil has made Mbasogo phenomenally wealthy. In two investigations conducted by the US Senate, it was found that oil companies deposit portions of Equatorial Guinea's oil revenue directly into accounts belonging to Mbasogo and his family. At one point, the balance in the president's account at the Riggs Bank in Washington, DC, was $700 million.

Mbasogo has so far proven more agreeable toward his family members than his uncle. His son, Teodoro Nguema Obiang Mangue, popularly called "Teodorin," lives a decadent playboy lifestyle packed with beautiful women and fast cars. As a dictator's son, he can generally consider Equatorial Guinea his own personal playground. When he wants to amuse himself with his many Ferraris or Bugattis, he orders streets closed in the capital, Mabako.

For many years, Teodorin was the minister of agriculture and forestry in Equatorial Guinea and therefore controlled the logging industry, the country's second most lucrative natural resource. Companies that want to log timber in Equatorial Guinea were required to pay large sums to Teodorin's own logging company. The official salary he received as minister was around $5,000 a month. Of course, his dictator-son lifestyle demands much more than that. According to the report from the US Senate, he has succeeded in amassing at least $100 million. In 2012, Teodorin was promoted to Second Vice President of Equatorial Guinea with special responsibility for defense and security.

In 1991, the twenty-two-year-old Teodorin traveled to the rich man's paradise of Malibu to study at Pepperdine University. Walter International, an American oil company, had agreed to pay the dictator son's living expenses. These quickly proved to be more than expected. Lodging was included in university tuition, but Teodorin wasn't satisfied with student housing. Instead, he rented an apartment in Malibu and a suite at the Beverly Wilshire Hotel in Los Angeles. Teodorin was seldom seen in class. He instead preferred to spend his time shopping in Beverly Hills. After five months, he dropped out of school altogether. Walter International was stuck with a $50,000 bill.

Though he didn't succeed in completing his studies, Teodorin liked California and continued to spend time there regularly. In 2001, he purchased a home in Bel Air for $6.5 million (though he didn't actually move in because he found the style too contemporary). In California, he also tried to build a career as a hip-hop mogul and founded the company TNO Entertainment. One of the albums he released was titled *No Better Than This*, with the rapper Won-G. Won-G, whose actual name is Wondgy Bruny, was a suitable partner. His father had been an officer in Haiti under dictator Jean-Claude Duvalier.

In 2006, Teodorin bought a mansion in Malibu for $30 million. The 15,000-square-foot mansion has eight bathrooms, a swimming pool, a tennis court, and a four-hole golf course. Mel Gibson and Britney Spears are among his neighbors. The US Senate report shows that when it came to furnishing, Teodorin spared no expense. He bought carpets totaling $59,850, a home cinema for $58,000, and a pair of wineglasses for $1,734.17.

According to the same report, Teodorin purchased a number of cars: seven Ferraris, five Bentleys, four Rolls-Royces, two Lamborghinis, two Mercedes, two Porsches, two Maybachs, and one Aston Martin. His favorite car was a blue Bugatti Veyron with a $2 million price tag. Benito Giacalone, a former chauffeur, has claimed that one time he parked the Bugatti outside a trendy nightclub. When Teodorin discovered that people had gathered around the car to admire it, he sent Giacalone home in a cab to fetch another Bugatti, which he wanted parked beside the first.

A host of women paraded through Teodorin's California mansion. Among others, he dated actress Tamala Jones, known from such movies as *Booty Call* and *Confessions of a Call Girl*; *Playboy* model Lindsey Evans; and rapper Eve. Teodorin made sure that both he and his female companions were elegantly dressed. The Dolce & Gabbana boutique closed its showroom when the dictator's son's girlfriends came to visit. According to Giacalone, one of them shopped for $80,000 worth of merchandise. The chauffeur paid with bundles of plastic-wrapped bills from a shoebox. In 2009, Teodorin spent a few nights in the Presidential Suite at the Four Seasons in Las Vegas. The $5,000 a night bill issued to Prince Teodoro Nguema Obiang leaves little doubt about his ideas on succession in Equatorial Guinea.

Despite his wealth, it appears that Teodorin often has difficulty paying the tab. Many of his employees have sued the heir for back compensation, overtime, and the cost of household expenditures, such as toilet paper. Former employees have also described his drug parties, escorts, and *Playboy* models: "I never witnessed him perform anything that looked like work. His days consisted entirely of sleeping, shopping, and partying," reads a statement from another former chauffeur.

Teodorin is frequently regarded as the most likely successor to Mbasogo. In recent years, he has spent more time in his homeland than abroad. It is unclear whether this is because he has started to take his political post more seriously or whether other factors are involved. After his economic activities were made public, it became more difficult for Teodorin to travel abroad, at least to some countries. In France, he has been charged with embezzlement and money laundering and at this writing is awaiting trial. A number of his luxury cars were confiscated by the French police in September 2011, and in February 2012, the police seized his mansion on the pricey Avenue Foch in Paris and confiscated valuables worth tens of millions of euros ($50 million for the furniture alone). The value of the house itself was estimated to be more than 170 million euros ($180 million) in 2012. In Switzerland, authorities seized luxury cars and asked Dutch authorities to seize his yacht *Ebony Shine*, worth $100 million. In 2014, federal prosecutors in the United States mounted a case against him that he settled by forfeiting his Malibu mansion, a Ferrari, and Michael Jackson memorabilia—though not the Swarovski-crystal-studded "Bad

Tour" glove worn by the singer on his first solo tour, which Teodorin managed to spirit out of the country.

Teodorin has been connected to another dictator's child, Princess Sikhanyiso, the daughter of King Mswati III of Swaziland, who is, according to *Forbes*, one of the world's twenty hottest young royals. Perhaps his relationship with Eve gave Teodorin a taste for musicians, for Sikhanyiso too has launched a musical career, partnering with the South African rapper Zuluboy. King Mswati and President Mbasogo are good friends and visit each other regularly. If these children of dictators find true love, two of Africa's most traditional dictatorships would celebrate even closer ties.

SEX, DRUGS, AND FAST CARS

When it comes to Arabian dictators, family members are famous for leading dissipated lives full of fast cars, beautiful women, and flowing champagne. In 2004, a sloshed Hannibal Gadhafi drove his black Porsche at eighty miles an hour—through a red light and on the wrong side of Champs-Élysées. When the police stopped Hannibal, six of his bodyguards showed up in another car and began to push and shove the officers. In February 2005, he beat up a friend when she tried to stop him from coming into her hotel room. The twenty-four-year-old model ended up hospitalized after the episode.

In the oil-rich countries of North Africa and the Middle East, absolute rulers have typically treated the state treasury as their own personal treasure box. A generation of princes have grown up in luxury beyond compare, above the law, and with the world at their feet. That has led to an endless chain of parties, model girlfriends, and scandals.

Few have filled the role of spoiled and decadent dictator offspring quite so successfully as Muammar Gadhafi's many sons. The Gadhafi family's bad boy is undoubtedly Hannibal, who got into so many squabbles with the French police that the Ministry of Foreign Affairs finally issued a warning to the Libyan authorities. They made it clear that Hannibal had no diplomatic immunity whatsoever—though the dictator's son tended to insist otherwise whenever he was arrested.

Those arrests were frequent. When the police showed up at the hotel after Hannibal's attack on his model friend in Paris, Hannibal reportedly began waving a pistol. The police succeeded in persuading him to drop it, whereupon Hannibal checked into the nearby hotel Royal Monceau. There he began destroying furniture, and the police were again called. Gadhafi declared he had diplomatic immunity, and the police left the scene. After the French Ministry of Foreign Affairs made it clear that the thirty-four-year-old could, in fact, be punished, Hannibal was tried and given a four-month suspended sentence.

The most significant crisis, however, came when Hannibal and his extremely pregnant wife were arrested in Switzerland for abusing two of their servants. Libya answered by shutting down Swiss companies in the country, arresting two Swiss businessmen, and throwing Swiss diplomats out of Libya. The authorities denied visas to Swiss citizens and threatened to stop oil exports.

In Tunisia, former president Zine El Abidine Ben Ali's son-in-law has distinguished himself as a socialite and playboy. Many assumed that Sakher El Materi, who is married to Ben

Ali's youngest daughter, was the president's designated successor. The American diplomatic correspondence published by
WikiLeaks provides insight into this Tunisian businessman's
extravagances: after a lunch with the president's son-in-law, the
American ambassador to Tunisia reported that ice cream and
frozen yogurt had been flown in from Saint Tropez, and the
host, like Saddam Hussein's son Uday, had a caged tiger.

El Materi's plans to assume power in Tunisia came to an
abrupt end when the country's people decided they had had
enough of the authoritarian and corrupt presidential family
and forced them to leave the country in January 2011. While
dictator offspring in North Africa act like royalty, a number of
princes farther east do their best to live up to their aristocratic
titles. In 2005, Sheikh Saud bin Saqr Al Qasimi, then crown
prince and now emir of Ras al-Khaimah, one of the United
Arab Emirates, was arrested in the United States for sexually
assaulting a housekeeper in his $5,000-a-night penthouse suite.
The prince was released after a weekend in custody, and he
immediately returned to his homeland.

For Sheikh Mohammed bin Sultan bin Mohammed Al
Qasimi, the eldest son of the emir of Sharjah, another of the
United Arab Emirates, the playboy lifestyle took a deadly turn.
In June 1999, the twenty-four-year-old was found dead in the
bathroom of his London home, with a strap around his arm and
syringes scattered around him. The prince had become addicted
to heroin after getting thrown out of an Arizona university.

In Saudi Arabia, the royal family has total control over the
country's politics and enormous oil wealth, which has guaranteed the many thousand princes a taste of the sweet life. Wah-
habism, the strict form of Islam that is Saudi Arabia's official
religion, may forbid alcohol and demand a puritanical lifestyle,

but apparently, that doesn't apply to royalty. Documents published by WikiLeaks describe a life of sex, drugs, and rock 'n' roll behind their closed doors.

A letter from the US consulate in Jeddah describes a Halloween party where alcohol and prostitutes abounded behind the heavily guarded gates of one prince's villa. The author points out that, even though drugs were not observed at the party, marijuana and cocaine are typical at this level of society. The document states: "Alcohol, though strictly prohibited by Saudi law and custom, was plentiful at the party's well-stocked bar. . . . The hired Filipino bartenders served a cocktail punch using 'sadiqi,' a locally-made 'moonshine.' . . . It was also learned through word-of-mouth that a number of the guests were in fact 'working girls,' not uncommon for such parties." The moral here is that no matter what rules apply to society in general, you are above them when you are related to a dictator.

Women, narcotics, and pet tigers seem like innocent fun compared to the darker side of some Arabian princes. In 2009, a video was smuggled out of the United Arab Emirates showing Sheikh Issa bin Zayed al Nahyan, the brother of Abu Dhabi's emir, torturing an Afghan businessman with the aid of a whip, a nail-studded board, and an electric branding iron. In the video, the victim is bound with tape while Sheikh Issa spreads salt on the wounds.

"The incidents depicted in the video tapes were not part of a pattern of behavior," declared the interior minister of the Emirates, who also happens to be one of Sheikh Issa's brothers. However, during the investigation, more than twenty-five other people brought accusations that they had also been filmed while being tortured by Sheikh Issa.

Prince Saud bin Abdulaziz bin Nasser al Saud, grandson of Saudi Arabia's King Abdullah, was sentenced in 2011 to life in prison in Great Britain for murdering his male servant. The two had been drinking champagne and Sex on the Beach cocktails in the bar at the five-star hotel in which they were staying before heading up to their room, where the servant was tortured to death. The prince had been brutalizing his servant for some time, and the hotel employees recounted that the man was treated like a slave. During the trial, it came to light that the two had engaged in a sexual relationship, and that the prince had also used male prostitutes. At that point, the prince and his lawyers spent more energy to disprove the homosexuality accusation than they did the murder charge, possibly because, in Saudi Arabia, homosexuality carries a death sentence. If the prince is ever freed in Great Britain, it is unlikely he will return to his homeland.

Even if Hannibal Gadhafi is perhaps the wildest of Colonel Gadhafi's sons, he is not the only family member with a taste for beautiful women and expensive champagne. On New Year's Eve in 2009, thirty-four-year-old Moutassim Billal Gadhafi was photographed at a private party on the Caribbean island of St. Barts. Pop star Beyoncé performed an hour-long concert for the guests, which included Bon Jovi, Jay-Z, Usher, and Lindsey Lohan.

Clearly, being a dictator is not just something you do for your own pleasure. It is also a gift to bestow on your nearest and dearest.

10

GET OUT IN TIME

IF YOU FOLLOW THE EXAMPLES described in the previous chapters, you will succeed as a dictator, and you will quickly discover that being a dictator has many advantages when compared to a democratically elected leader. Dictators often occupy power longer than heads of state in democratic countries. During your tenure, you can make yourself filthy rich, be worshipped like a god, and allow yourself to become drunk on power. However, there is one thing all dictators must keep in mind: your political career can end at the drop of a hat. Therefore, you must be prepared.

If you succeed in maintaining power without falling victim to a coup or an assassination attempt, you have two possibilities. You can either keep your post until you die, or you can choose to step down and let someone else take over. Given the choice, most dictators remain in power until death. There are many reasons for this. In a monarchy, the king, emir, sultan, or prince is naturally the head of state for life. When monarchs die or become too old or sick to attend to their daily duties, the next in line takes over, although the monarch will usually retain his title until death.

For other dictators, the situation is somewhat different. To step down as state leader can have serious consequences. You could be accused of corruption, abuse of human rights, nepotism, election fraud, and for coming to power through unlawful means. A dictator who voluntarily retires thus runs the risk of being charged with and prosecuted for crimes committed during his tenure as head of state. After all, there are always petty and jealous people who will not feel that their interests were duly safeguarded during your reign.

In addition, when a dictator throws in the towel, there is always the danger of a power struggle. As a rule, a number of people stand ready and willing to assume power. The populace may seize the opportunity and revolt. Therefore, it may be wise to handpick and groom a successor. However, even if you do choose your successor, you can never be entirely certain that person is loyal. You might find yourself with a knife in the back.

Retirement being a risky gamble for a dictator, few take the chance. Instead of remaining in their homeland, many dictators prefer a retirement-like lifestyle in a friendly foreign country. A change of climate is appealing in itself, even though, for a dictator, the political climate is always the most important.

One dictatorial rule of thumb is to never admit your mistakes. Everything you did was for the good of the people. Accusations of murder, torture, and human rights abuses can always be dismissed as lies. Alternatively, you can claim that you had no choice, as the Polish communist dictator Wojciech Jaruzelski did after communism's fall: "If I am guilty, then so is a whole generation. Anyone in my position would have done the same."

Another variant is to claim that you were at war, as did Ethiopia's dictator Mengistu Haile Mariam. At present, Mariam is a permanent guest of his dictator colleague Robert Mugabe in Zimbabwe. As Mariam states, "I'm a military man. I did what I did only because my country had to be saved from tribalism and feudalism. If I failed, it was only because I was betrayed. The so-called genocide was nothing more than just a war in defense of the revolution and a system from which all have benefited." You can also do as Emperor Jean-Bédel Bokassa did and blame international politics: "I didn't obey France. And for that they stripped me of power."

Ex-dictators cannot always travel where their fancy takes them. Many countries refuse to accept them—some even threaten indictment—and others will send you straight back to your homeland. Luckily, though, there are countries that stand ready to embrace you with open arms. France was long a dream destination for dethroned dictators, especially those from former French colonies. One of those who traveled to France was his Imperial Highness Jean-Bédel Bokassa from the Central African Empire. In 1979, as we learned above, more than one hundred schoolchildren and university students were killed after protesting having to buy expensive school uniforms. Allegedly, Bokassa himself participated in the children's abuse. France decided to remove Bokassa from power. While the emperor was visiting Gadhafi in Libya, French troops launched Operation Barracuda on September 20, 1979. The French reinstated David Dacko, who had occupied power before Bokassa's 1966 coup. (Naturally, Dacko had been living in exile in France.)

Bokassa fled first to the Ivory Coast, where he was installed in Villa Cocody, in one of Abidjan's finer neighborhoods. The Ivory Coast's president, Félix Houphouët-Boigny, made certain the ex-emperor received warm meals from a hotel twice a day. In Abidjan, Bokassa spent his time listening to a record of military marches played by the French navy's brass orchestra. He attempted to arrange asylum with his old friend Muammar Gadhafi, but the Libyan dictator had his hands full with Idi Amin, who had just been booted from Uganda.

A few years later, Bokassa moved to Paris, where he succeeded in creating a small scandal when he attempted to publish his memoir. In the book, Bokassa claims that the French president, Valéry Giscard d'Estaing, who was a frequent visitor to the Central African Republic, slept with the same girls he did. He also insists that in 1973, when Giscard was minister of foreign affairs, he gave Giscard diamonds worth $250,000. Giscard lost the next presidential election, probably because of the scandal. Unfortunately, no one got to read the book—all eight thousand copies were shredded on orders from a French court.

Another dictator who traveled to France was Jean-Claude "Baby Doc" Duvalier, who had been in power since his father's death in 1971. At the beginning of the 1980s, dissatisfaction began to spread among Haiti's populace. In the fall of 1985, a revolt began, at which point Baby Doc saw that his time was up. In Gonaïves, a group of revolutionaries arranged Baby Doc's burial, complete with coffins and human bones. One gravestone read "Jon Clod Min Place Ou"—"Jean-Claude, This Is Your Place." Duvalier left Haiti on February 8, 1986, and set a course for France. He actually preferred America, but the United States had refused to give him political asylum. France did not want the deposed dictator either but gave him a week-long residence permit in the hopes that another country would take him. None would.

Duvalier and his wife, Michelle, rented a house on the French Riviera and moved in with their two children. In an ironic twist of fate, his neighbor was the British author Graham Greene, who wrote *The Comedians*, a satirical novel about Duvalier's father, François "Papa Doc" Duvalier, and his rule in Haiti.

Baby Doc had sent enormous sums out of his country in the course of his tenure ($900 million, according to Haiti's estimate), but most of the money has mysteriously vanished. Multiple bank accounts in Switzerland and Great Britain were frozen at the request of Haitian authorities, but they contained only a fraction of the amount he apparently tucked away. A partial explanation is that Michelle received a significant portion of Duvalier's fortune when the couple divorced in 1993. Michelle had wielded strict control of the family's finances ever since she had married Baby Doc.

By 1994, Baby Doc was broke. At one point, he couldn't even pay the rent. France Telecom disconnected his telephone. He moved from one place to another and lived out of a suitcase with his new partner, Veronique Roy. Roy is the granddaughter of Paul Magloire, Haiti's president from 1950 to 1956, but she had never been to Haiti when she began dating the ex-president. On January 16, 2011, shortly after a powerful earthquake struck the country, Baby Doc traveled back to Haiti. He claimed it was to help his countrymen, certainly not to reclaim power or to get his hands on a money stash. Two days later he was arrested and accused of corruption, embezzlement, and theft. He was released a short time later but was not allowed to leave Haiti. Many Haitians accused him of torture and human rights abuses, but he died in 2014, forever evading criminal charges.

Valentine Strasser had come to power in Sierra Leone more or less by happenstance in 1992. On January 16, 1996, he left the capital of Freetown in order to review a military parade at the military academy in Benguema. He returned to Freetown that same afternoon to participate in a meeting at defense headquarters. There he was arrested, shoved into a helicopter, and flown straight to Conakry in neighboring Guinea, just as Strasser had had done with his predecessor, Joseph Momoh, four years earlier. His second-in-command, Julias Maada Bio, took over as president.

Of course, Strasser himself maintains that he was no coup victim but willingly resigned after having concluded ten years of military service. As part of peace negotiations in Sierra Leone, one-time members of the military junta were allowed to study in Great Britain. Strasser received the same offer, even though he had already been deposed.

In England, Strasser studied law at Warwick University but gave up in 1998 because he was tired of seeing the headlines in newspapers declaring him a former dictator and responsible for human rights abuses. He moved to London, but after the *Guardian* newspaper questioned why a previous dictator was allowed to live in England, he returned to Gambia, and to his homeland shortly thereafter.

Now the former dictator lives with his mother in rural Grafton, right outside of Freetown. During the afternoon, he often sits on the terrace sipping gin from a plastic cup. His disco-dancing days are over, and he has to subsist on the forty-six dollars a month Sierra Leone gives him as pension.

WELCOME TO THE JUNGLE

If Baby Doc had stood trial in Haiti and was condemned for the crimes of which he is accused, he would have become part of an exclusive group of dictators. Few dictators actually end up behind bars. One of the more unfortunate members of this group, who has bounced between jails in various countries and will probably spend the rest of his life behind bars, is Manuel Noriega. Noriega received military training in the United States and for a long time had two simultaneous careers: one as a CIA agent and one as drug smuggler for the notorious Medellin cartel. In 1983, he declared himself general and became Panama's de facto dictator, even though Ricardo de la Espriella Toral was technically president at the time.

Noriega had apparently forgotten a couple of lessons in election fraud. During the presidential election in May 1989, the number of tampered ballots was so massive that Noriega's candidate, Carlos Duque, realized he had been decisively defeated and refused to be inaugurated as president. Noriega was forced to void the entire election.

A number of confrontations between the United States and Panama in the following months led to the US invasion of Panama on December 20 of that same year. Noriega sought sanctuary at the Vatican's embassy, whereupon American troops surrounded the embassy and began blasting music around the clock, including Van Halen's "Panama" and Guns N' Roses' "Welcome to the Jungle." On January 3, 1990, the dictator had had enough and surrendered. In 1992, he was sentenced to forty years of imprisonment for drug smuggling, organized crime, and money laundering. The sentence was later reduced to thirty years.

In 2000, the Italian journalist Riccardo Orizio requested an interview with Noriega, who at that time was jailed in Florida, and received the following answer: "With reference to your request for an interview in connection with a projected book about certain 'forgotten individuals,' once-powerful people who have been blamed for the problems encountered by their respective countries, etc., my response is that I do not consider myself to be a 'forgotten individual,' because God, the great Creator of the universe, He who writes straight albeit with occasionally crooked lines, has not yet written the last word on MANUEL A. NORIEGA!"

He was right. The last word on Manuel A. Noriega had yet to be written. After the former dictator was released from prison in 2007 (Noriega's sentence had been significantly reduced due to good behavior), several new trials awaited him, including one in France. France had sentenced him in absentia to ten years' imprisonment for money laundering. Like many other dictators, Noriega had harbored a fondness for France and had laundered drug money by purchasing apartments in Paris. The ex-dictator was extradited to France to be tried anew. This time, Noriega was sentenced to seven years' imprisonment, and the 2.3 million euros he stashed in French bank accounts were confiscated.

In 1995, Noriega was sentenced in absentia to twenty years' imprisonment for murder and human rights abuses in Panama. In December 2011, at seventy-seven years old, he was extradited to Panama for a new round of trials. There is little hope the aging ex-dictator will experience a life beyond bars.

Another dictator who has been sentenced to imprisonment is Liberia's Charles Taylor. On April 26, 2012, he was found guilty on eleven counts of war crimes and crimes against humanity.

However, Manuel Noriega and Charles Taylor are exceptions. In general, most dictators succeed in negotiating for exile upon resigning from power.

The unfortunate fact of the matter is that many dictators are also killed in the line of duty. There is no doubt that being a dictator is a dangerous profession. As we have seen, Francisco Macías Nguema of Equatorial Guinea was sentenced to death 101 times and executed. Libya's Muammar Gadhafi was killed while fleeing from rebels, and pictures of his bloody corpse were broadcast on TV the world over. The Ceauşescus were hauled away in December 1989 when their ungrateful subjects turned against them. Following a short trial, they were executed by firing squad on December 25, 1989.

After more than thirty years in power, the Dominican Republic's Rafael Trujillo had accumulated quite a few enemies. The Kennedy administration in Washington, DC, wanted to see him gone; the CIA tried to find ways of removing him; and the Dominican Republic's elite were fed up with decades of brutal repression. However, it was a handful of Trujillo's own subordinates who finally took matters into their own hands.

Trujillo went out in pure Mafioso style on May 30, 1961. The dictator had been to visit his daughter, Angelita, and was on his way to Bar Restaurante El Pony. On a road outside the capital, Ciudad Trujillo, the car was ambushed. The attackers peppered the vehicle with bullets. The wounded dictator climbed out of the car to shoot back but was met by a hail of bullets and was killed. His corpse was stuffed into the trunk of a Chevrolet. The four ambushers were members of the army, and the plotters included a couple of generals. The plan was to seize power in the Dominican Republic, yet some of the assassins' collaborators were reluctant to reveal themselves before they had seen Trujillo's body, and it was too dangerous to transport the corpse through a city packed with police and security forces. If El Jefe had survived, they knew, any coup attempt would be doomed. Consequently, the coup floundered. After first being buried in Trujillo's hometown of San Cristóbal, his corpse was later taken to Paris, but it was eventually moved to a churchyard outside the Spanish capital Madrid.

Sometimes the past catches up with dictators who have abandoned their posts and fled into exile. Anastasio "Tachito" Somoza Debayle assumed power in Nicaragua after his brother, Luis Anastasio Somoza Debayle, died in 1967. Luis, in turn, had inherited the position of dictator from his father, Anastasio "Tacho" Somoza García. Altogether, the Somoza family governed Nicaragua from 1936 to 1979. At one point, Franklin D. Roosevelt was quoted as remarking in 1939 that "[Tacho] Somoza may be a son of a bitch, but he's our son of a bitch." The expression has since been attributed to a number of American administrations, with Somoza's name being replaced by other US-friendly dictators. Some believe that Somoza himself spread the myth of Roosevelt's quip.

Throughout the 1970s, Tachito lost American support and most of what the government had in the form of international backing. In 1979, the Sandinistas, Nicaragua's resistance movement, succeeded in hounding Somoza out of the land. He flew first to Miami, but was refused by American authorities and was forced to travel, tail between his legs, to fellow dictator Alfredo Stroessner in Paraguay, where he was welcomed with open arms. He bought a farm and a villa in the capital of Asuncíon and prepared to live the retired lifestyle.

However, the Sandinistas had no intention of letting Somoza remain in peace. Under the code name "Operation Reptile," they planned to assassinate the former dictator. On September 17, 1979, they set out, armed with two Kalashnikov AK-47 machine guns, two pistols, and a handful of rocket-propelled grenades. The assassins concealed themselves and waited for Somoza to leave his house in his Mercedes. The first grenade failed, so the assassins shot the chauffeur and reloaded the grenade launcher. The second grenade struck its target. Somoza and two other passengers were immediately reduced to charred residue. The ex-dictator was so thoroughly annihilated, he had to be identified by his feet during the autopsy. Just one assassin, Hugo Irarzun, was captured. Six others escaped.

Many dictators have died under mysterious circumstances. Of course, a dictator dying is often a mystery in and of itself. In any case, it is enough to give rise to myths and speculations, for no dictator lacks enemies or rivals. Sani Abacha is a dictator whose death has been the subject of much speculation. As a career officer in Nigeria since 1963, Abacha had a hand in a number of military coups. After he achieved power in 1993, he became known as the most corrupt head of state of his day.

On June 8, 1998, he died in the presidential residence located in Nigeria's capital of Abuja. The official cause of death was a heart attack, but the deceased dictator was buried, according to Islamic tradition, the same day as he died—without an autopsy. What is certain is that the morning he died, he was in the company of a handful of Indian prostitutes, six of them apparently imported straight from Dubai. These circumstances have given rise to the speculation that he might have been poisoned. Other people believe that, given the dictator's state of heath, it is not improbable that the situation did lead to his heart giving out.

Abacha's utterly deceived wife Maryam was arrested at Lagos's airport with thirty-eight suitcases full of foreign currency that totaled up to $100 million.

DICTATORS AS DECOR

Some countries have a tradition of pickling their dictators. The trend started with the Soviet dictator Vladimir Lenin, who was stuffed after he died in 1924. Some people also suggested cryogenically freezing Lenin's body in order to revive him when medical advances were far enough along. Equipment was even purchased for the purpose, but the Soviet authorities chose to simply preserve the body and put it on display. Lenin is still on display in a mausoleum in Moscow's Red Square. Periodically, he must be bathed in embalming fluid, and to keep his skin from blackening, he must be treated with a variety of different applications during the baths. It has been said that a number of Lenin's body parts have been replaced by artificial ones.

Chairman Mao Zedong wanted to be cremated. Nonetheless, when he died in 1976, the Chinese decided to embalm him. Unfortunately, they began the process too late, and Mao's doctor, who was given the task, had never embalmed a body before. For security's sake, he injected double the amount of formaldehyde required, and Mao ended up looking like the Michelin Man. In order to repair the damage, the doctors massaged the body to squeeze the liquid out, but that caused Mao's face to fall off. It was then repaired with wax. According to rumor, it is a wax figure, not Mao himself, who is on display in Beijing.

Other dictators who have been stuffed are Ferdinand Marcos, Kim Il Sung, Bulgaria's Georgi Dimitrov, and Czechoslovakia's Klement Gottwald. The Argentinean dictator Juan Perón decided that his wife, Eva (better known as Evita), would be embalmed when she died in 1952. She was filled with glycerol and put on display in his office. Perón's plan was to build a mausoleum and monument bigger than the Statue of Liberty to honor her. Unfortunately, Perón fell victim to a coup in 1955 before the mausoleum could be completed. Evita's corpse disappeared but was discovered in a Milan crypt in 1971. She was reunited with her husband, who was then living in exile in Spain with his new wife. The couple kept the corpse in the dining room, which easily could have led to a bizarre love triangle. Evita was finally sent back to Argentina and buried in the family grave in Buenos Aires.

All this is to say that on the one hand, there are certain dangers associated with becoming a dictator. On the other, you have much to gain should all go right. And remember, few democratically elected politicians occupy power as long as the world's longest-reigning dictators. Paul Biya has been in power in Cameroon since 1975; Teodoro Nguema Obiang Mbasogo has governed Equatorial Guinea since 1979; Zimbabwe's Robert Mugabe has been state head since 1980; in Uganda, Yoweri Museveni has been president since 1986. Indeed, some royal autocrats govern even longer. Hassanal Bolkiah of Brunei inherited the throne in 1967, and Sultan Qaboos of Oman came to power in 1970.

If you succeed as dictator, you are guaranteed a life filled with excitement, unlimited power, a population that worships you like a god, and, most of all, fantastic wealth. Take the word of Uganda's president, Yoweri Museveni, who pointed out the magnificent advantages associated with dictatorship. In 1988, the Ugandan dictator received notable publicity when he blamed his African colleagues for occupying power too long.

"The problem of Africa in general, and Uganda in particular, is not the people but leaders who want to overstay in power," he said. By February 2012, however, he had changed his tune. In a speech, he proclaimed, "Some people think that being in government for a long time is a bad thing. But the more you stay, the more you learn. I am now an expert in governance."

BIBLIOGRAPHY

Bueno de Mesquita, Bruno, and Alastair Smith. *The Dictator's Handbook: Why Bad Behavior Is Almost Always Good Politics.* New York: PublicAffairs, 2011.

Cawthorne, Nigel. *Sex Lives of the Great Dictators.* London: Prion, 2004.

Derby, Lauren. *The Dictator's Seduction: Politics and the Popular Imagination in the Era of Trujillo.* Durham, NC: Duke University Press, 2009.

Diederich, Bernhard and Al Burt. *Papa Doc & the Tontons Macoutes.* Princeton, NJ: Markus Wiener Publishers, 2005.

Gadhafi, Muammar. *The Green Book.* Reading, UK: Ithaca Press, 2005.

Gadhafi, Muammar. *Escape To Hell and Other Stories.* London: Blake Publishing Ltd., 1999.

Hebditch, David, and Ken Connor. *How to Stage a Military Coup.* London: Greenhill Books, 2005.

Holland, Heidi. *Dinner With Mugabe: The Untold Story of a Freedom Fighter who Became a Tyrant.* New York: Penguin Books, 2008.

Hussein, Saddam. *Zabibah and the King.* Virtualbookworm. com, 2004.

Il Sung, Kim. *Sea of Blood.* 1971.

Jong Il, Kim. *On the Art of the Cinema.* Honolulu: University Press of the Pacific, 2001.

Jong Il, Kim. *On the Art of the Opera.* Honolulu: University Press of the Pacific, 2001.

Kinzer, Stephen. *A Thousand Hills: Rwanda's Rebirth and the Man Who Dreamed It.* New York: Wiley, 2008.

Luttwak, Edward. *Coup d'Etat: A Practical Handbook.* London: Allen Lane, 1968.

Myers, B. R. *The Cleanest Race: How North Koreans See Themselves—And Why It Matters.* New York: Melville House, 2010.

Niyazov, Saparmurat. *Ruhnama.* Ashkaban: State Publishing Service of Turkmenistan, 2003.

Orizio, Riccardo. *Talk of the Devil: Encounters with Seven Dictators.* New York: Walker Books, 2004.

Shaw, Karl. *The Little Book of Loony Dictators.* Sensible Shoes, 2011.

Titley, Brian. *Dark Age: The Political Odyssey of Emperor Bokassa.* Montreal and Kingston, Canada: McGill–Queen's University Press, 1997.

Wrong, Michela. *In the Footsteps of Mr. Kurtz: Living on the Brink of Disaster in Mobuto's Congo.* New York: HarperCollins, 2001.

York, Peter. *Dictator Style: Lifestyles of the World's Most Colorful Despots.* Chronicle Books, 2006.